The Sanson Family Tree

Marie-Josèphe m. her cousin Jean-Louis	A son executioner of Blois	A daughter m. the executioner of Etampes	A daughter m. the executioner of Meaux	A son executioner of Rennes	A son executioner of Montpellier	A son executioner of Orleans
One daughter						

NOTE

The name Sanson is very widespread; bearers of this name are not necessarily descendants of the famous dynasty of executioners.

Relationship between the Paris executioners is indicated by thick black lines.

THE EXECUTIONERS

THE
EXECUTIONERS

A History of the Sanson Family, Public Executioners
in France from 1688 to 1847

by

ROBERT CHRISTOPHE

Translated from the French
by Len Ortzen

ARTHUR BARKER LIMITED

20 NEW BOND STREET LONDON W 1

To the fine painter, Clotilde Avy-Prégniard,
to whom I owe the idea for this book

R.C.

PRINTED IN HOLLAND BY
LEVISSON PRESS, THE HAGUE.
27/5222

Contents

Five names on a tombstone

ONE AFTERNOON, the author of this book was trying to escape from the noises of Paris by seeking quiet in Montmartre cemetery. But it was only on reaching the 20th sector that he was able to hear the whisper of the breeze, the chirping of sparrows in the trees, and the fall of a few raindrops left on the leaves from a recent shower. At last he could wander at leisure.

As he went along the Artot pathway he felt he would like to have another look at the grave of Louis XVI's executioner. He knew of it, as eight years earlier he had sought it out in connection with some literary work. Even at a distance he could make out the inscription on the base of the tomb: SANSON FAMILY.

As on the previous occasion, his mind dwelt on the martyred King and the ill-fated Queen. He went up to the humble family grave, one of the oldest in the cemetery, for it bears the number twenty-seven. A metal railing encloses it, broken in several places by rust. The solitary walker could tell by the dirt and moss around the tomb that no one now came to visit it.

He leant against the rusty railing, and tried to decipher the names carved on the headstone surmounted by a small cross. He had to take his handkerchief and wipe away the dirt and muck encrusted in the lettering by the wind and rain. It was not easy, but the words were at last revealed. And this is what he read, omitting the inevitable trite expressions of regret:

Charles-Henri SANSON
born in Paris on February 15th, 1739.
passed away on July 4th, 1806.
Henri SANSON

born in Paris on December 24th, 1767,
passed away on August 18th, 1840.
Virginie-Emilie LEFEBURE
SANSON by marriage
died on March 29th, 1860,
in her 62nd year.
Marie-Louise DAMIDOT
widow of Henri SANSON
born in Paris on October 14th, 1776,
died June 18th, 1866.
Henri-Clément SANSON
died January 25th, 1889,
aged 89.

Five bodies had been laid to rest below this modest tombstone
— three husbands, but only two of their wives. Curious to know
where the third wife was buried, the profaner of the neglected
tombstone went and consulted the cemetery registers, but found
no trace of the wife of Charles-Henri Sanson. There was another
surprise: on some manuscript sheets kept in the same building an
entry relating to Henri Sanson gave him as having succeeded his
father in 1793, and not on July 4th, 1806, the date of demise
carved on the tombstone. What was the reason for this anomaly?

Returning pensively to the 20th sector, the author of this book
remembered a retort in Victor Hugo's 'Mary Tudor': *Joshua* —
'Mind you, Gilbert, the man who knows the history of these
times best is the turnkey at the Tower of London.' *Simon Renard,*
coming on — 'You're mistaken, master, it's the executioner!'

For the three men buried in tomb number twenty-seven had,
between them, held by the hair the heads of Louis XVI and Marie
Antoinette, of Lucile Desmoulins, Robespierre, Lesurques, Cadoudal, Louvel, and the four sergeants from La Rochelle, of
Fieschi, Lacenaire, and of several thousand persons of both sexes
who, with pen and sword, had figured in a hundred years of
French history.

Many writers go to Italy, Greece, or Spain in search of inspiration.

More is often found in a Paris cemetery. The author of this book, having the last resting-place of the Sansons before his eyes, felt the urge to set down their life-stories. His first researches were at the Bibliothèque Nationale. One thing leading to another, from printed 'Memoirs' to manuscript sources, he gradually unearthed material of use to his project.

At first, the books he found were disappointing. There was *Memoirs relative to the history of the French Revolution, by Sanson, executioner of criminal sentences.* This work, published in 1829, was apocryphal. It had been put together by Balzac and L'héritier de l'Ain, and portrayed characters belonging more to a novel than to real life.

Then there was *Memoirs of the public executioner, of use to the history of Paris during the Terror.* Alas, the author of this volume published in 1830 was a certain A. Grégoire, and it was nothing but a mixture of anecdotes culled from the tittle-tattle of the Revolutionary period.

Finally came *The Memoirs of the Sansons (Seven generations of executioners), arranged and edited by H. Sanson, ex-public executioner to the Paris courts.* This time, the searcher's heart beat faster. Unfortunately, he had only to begin reading the six interminable volumes, published in 1862, for his joy to turn to doubt. Here are the opening paragraphs, attributed to the pen of the last Sanson to be laid to rest in the Montmartre family grave, Henri-Clément:

'On March 18th, 1847, I was returning home tired out by one of those long walks during which I sought lonely places to bury my gloomy thoughts and constant obsessions. Hardly had I entered the courtyard, and the ancient gate which was so rarely opened had swung heavily back, squeaking on its rusty hinges, than the concierge handed me a letter.

'I immediately recognised the large folded paper and that large seal whose aspect had always made me shudder with dismay and grief; I took the missive with trembling hand and, expecting to find it contained one of those dismal orders which my terrible position obliged me to obey, I went painfully up the steps into the house.

'When I reached my office I despairingly broke open this fateful letter. It informed me I was relieved of my post!

'A strange, indefinable feeling came over me. I looked up at the portraits of my forbears; my eyes wandered over those sombre, contemplative faces, on each of which could be read the same thoughts as had blighted my existence until then; I gazed at my grandfather (Charles-Henri, the executioner of Louis XVI) dressed for going shooting, leaning dismally on the barrel of his gun ... I gazed at my father (Henri, the executioner of Marie-Antoinette) holding his hat in his hand and dressed in the lugubrious mourning clothes that he always wore. It seemed to me that I was letting all these silent onlookers know of the end of the fatality which had weighed upon their race, and was associating them with what I was about to do.

'I pulled at a bell-rope and had a wash-bowl and some water brought up to me. And there, alone before God who can see into the depths of human hearts, I solemnly washed these hands that the blood of my fellow-beings would stain no more.

'Then I went to see my mother (Marie-Louise Damidot, the fourth name on the tombstone), a humble, saintly woman — for we did find women to marry us!

'I can still see her sitting there in her Dutch-velvet-covered armchair, from which it was difficult for her to rise. I placed the missive from the Minister for Justice on her lap. She read it; then, turning towards me her kind eyes from which I had so often drawn all my courage and strength, she said, 'Blessed be this day, my son! At last, the foul part of your inheritance from your fathers is lifted from you.'

Continuing in this emphatic tone, Henri-Clément then recalled his conversation with the old lady. He mentioned his daughters, and the thanks he gave to Heaven for taking from him his son, *the last of his race;* and the 18 competitors wanting to be his 'bloodstained successor'. He added these enigmatic lines:

'As for me, I hastened to sell this old house which was full of such sad memories, and where seven generations of my family had lived, penned in by opprobrium and ignominy; and my horses, my carriage on which was painted *a cracked bell* — as a pictorial coat-of-arms — instead of an escutcheon dating from the crusades... Then, shaking the dust from my feet, I left for ever this family dwelling where, like my ancestors, I had not been able to enjoy peaceful days nor restful nights.'

What was this 'cracked bell' which took the place of an escutcheon dating from the crusades?

The writer of the 'Memoirs', as he was presumed to be, maintained he was a descendant of a Sanson de Longval, seneschal of Robert the Magnificent, the father of William the Conqueror and a valiant fighter in the Holy Land. This 'banneret of the Dukes of Normandy' is certainly mentioned in the chronicles of Villehardouin and Joinville. So the last of the notorious public executioners could pride himself — if he was not lying — on having an 'escutcheon dating from the crusades.' As for the 'cracked bell' that took its place on his carriage, a pun on words appeared with it — Sans son (No sound).

Whether there was any truth or not in this ancient, noble origin of the family, the extracts reproduced above certainly give cause for reflection. Their author does not appear at all like a legendary torturer. He shows himself to be sensitive and human, filled with repugnance for his office. The style of writing is more that of someone used to pushing a pen than of a public executioner. He deemed it advisable, nevertheless, to assert in his preface:

'It has perhaps been thought that I picked out of the gutter-press some cheap hack to compose a book under my name, and this gave rise to the indignation and jeers directed against the book even before its appearance. Readers will soon perceive that it is a sincere, authentic work, and one that could only germinate in the mind of a man worn by the sufferings that have been my natural lot.'

That remains to be seen...

These 'Memoirs of the Sansons' swarm with inaccuracies, and there are lots of more or less deliberate omissions. Moreover, long after publication it was learnt that the author had only written a part of the book. Most of the work, for which he had provided the material, was done not by one hack but by two. The chief one was a journalist by the name of d'Olbreuse. The name of the other is not known; he was no doubt a writer of some reputation who had fallen on hard times and was reduced to this mean task for a living. The publisher, Dupray de la Mahérie, paid the ex-public executioner 30,000 francs, and d'Olbreuse 17,500. It is not known how much the other ghost-writer received.

In 1908 the celebrated historian, G. Lenotre, mentioned this arrangement in his book, *La Guillotine pendant La Révolution*, and declared that d'Olbreuse paid 12,500 francs of his fee to his anonymous collaborator, keeping only 5,000 for himself. Wherever did Lenotre get this piece of information? According to him, from 'one of my colleagues' who had seen Sanson 'during those odd negotiations'. Lenotre does not seem to have delved very deeply into matters that took him away from the main subject of his book. Thus he admits, in connection with the executioner of Louis XVI,' I have been unable to find an entry of his death in public records.' He had but to go and consult the archives of the three large Paris cemeteries; he would have discovered Charles-Henri's grave in Montmartre cemetery and the date, July 4th, 1806, carved on the tombstone.

Lenotre was hardly any nearer the mark over the death of Charles-Henri's grandson, the accredited author of the 'Memoirs'. In the same book on *La Guillotine* he wrote of the last of the Sansons: 'He died about fifteen years ago.' This camouflaged avowal of ignorance was printed in 1908 — when for nearly twenty years the date of January 25th, 1889, had been on the tombstone.

Another writer, considered a specialist in judicial and penal subjects, repeated Lenotre's mistake. In a highly documented book on Deibler, public executioner during the Third Republic, M. Paul Dornain devoted several pages to Charles-Henri Sanson and there wrote (this was in 1934): 'It is not known when the executioner of Louis XVI died.'

And then there are novels written around the notorious dynasty of executioners by two or three literary men. For lack of documentation, everything in these books is invented, even the Christian names of the wives of some of those gentlemen.

All of which shows how obscure and difficult the history of the Sanson family appears.

Besides, the three men buried in the Montmartre grave were not the only Sansons to have 'performed the sinister tasks thrust upon them by birth'. The names of earlier generations appear in judicial records: Charles Sanson, called Charles I; his son, Charles, called Charles II; the third in the line, Charles-Jean-Baptiste, and his seven offspring, who all became public executioners, as did his three sons-in-law. The eldest of that large family was the Charles-Henri destined to guillotine Louis XVI, and whose mortal remains were the first to be laid in the family grave. So that from 1635 — when Charles I was born — until January 25th, 1889, the day Henri-Clément passed away, six generations of Sansons wielded the sword of justice. And not seven, as the sub-title of the *Memoirs of the Sansons* falsely claims. Though, admittedly, d'Olbreuse and his anonymous collaborator were including Charles I's father-in-law, Pierre Jouenne, who was public executioner at Dieppe.

These earlier Sansons were buried in a family vault in the church of St. Laurent, which stands at the corner of the present Boulevard de Strasbourg and Boulevard de Magenta, just south of the Gare de l'Est.

As holders of a monopoly which they were never able to abandon, the Sansons had a part in the history of France from the time of Louis XIV to that of Louis-Philippe. Throughout almost two centuries, they pilloried, whipped, branded, hanged, broke on the wheel or beheaded their fellow human-beings of both sexes. Though actually they rarely took an active part themselves, but directed the operations of their many assistants.

The earlier Sansons were wealthy; they invited people to dinner, they gave parties and fêtes, and were far from shrinking from contact with the world, although their name was covered with shame. They considered themselves auxiliaries of the law as much as magistrates, and took to court anyone who insulted them. But after the French Revolution, when there remained only the guillotine for them to work, the Sansons found their importance considerably reduced. When the liberal-minded 19th century rejected the death penalty and induced juries to be more merciful, the Sansons fell into a situation bordering on poverty. The last of them faced ruin, and to complete his misfortune was notified of his dismissal. Later, he had the *Memoirs of the Sansons* put together, that family chronicle which appeared in 1862 and sold more than 80,000 copies. In it, as mentioned above, he claimed to be of noble descent.

On the other hand, the concoction produced by A. Grégoire in 1830 (also previously mentioned) put the following words into the mouth of Henri-Clément's grandfather:

'The first Sanson who devoted his life to punishing the guilty, Pietro Sansoni — for he was an Italian — was drawn into this career of reprobation by sentiments that were heroic for the times he lived in, and by a succession of frightful circumstances.'

That was going back six centuries, and according to the author proof of it appeared later, in 1635, when a Sanson was 'the executioner appointed by the Duc de Lorges, high justiciary of France under Louis XIII.'

Pure imagination! This Duc de Lorges was born in 1630, and he could hardly have become Minister of Justice at the age of five! In that year, 1635, Charles Sanson had only just come into the world. To hang people while still sucking at the breast would have been an unusual feat. His father, a tradesman at Abbeville, had just died during an epidemic. Moreover, Monsieur de Lorges was not created duke until 1676, for the part he played during the retreat of Turenne's armies. And the list of public executioners for Paris in the reign of Louis XIII only gives the names of Jean Guillaume and Nicolas Levasseur, known as La Rivière. So this tale of the Italian origin of the Sansons must be regarded as a fable.

The author of this present book has read, analysed, and dissected the bulky 'Memoirs' edited by the last of the notorious line of executioners. He has compared the six volumes with all the documents which, for the past 350 years, have had some connection with the Sansons. So the story he gives in the following pages, while not pretending to be the final pronouncement, is the closest possible to what might be called the historical truth.

CHAPTER ONE

Public executioner through love

ABOUT TWELVE MILES north-west of Péronne, in the Somme *département,* is the small village of Longueval. In the 17th century its name was spelt Longval. The population then barely numbered three hundred. The taxes they paid went to swell the Royal Treasury, church funds, and the purse of a vassal authorised by his overlord to collect these revenues. This concessionary of the little fief was of minor or doubtful nobility, and his name was Sanson. Which was why he called himself Sanson de Longval.

He lived some fifty miles away from his tenure, in the ancient town of Abbeville on the river Somme. In those days, the estuary not then being silted up, small ships came right up to Abbeville to discharge and load cargoes, as the name of more than one street testifies today. The town supplied Paris with fish, with wine brought by sea from the south of France, with spices from Arabia, and furs and timber from Scandinavia. Abbeville had a flourishing trade, and the burghers lived well.

Although making himself out to be seigneur of Longval, as he pocketed a third of its taxes, Master Sanson soiled his hands with the shipping trade of his fellow-townsmen. His wife — whose maiden name was Brossier — had borne him two children at an interval of eleven years: Jean-Baptiste in 1624, and Charles in 1635.

While the two boys were still young they lost both their parents in an epidemic, and were given a home by their uncle, Pierre Brossier. He, too, was a burgher of Abbeville and played at being a seigneur. He had the charge of the fief of Limeux and collected its taxes. He was a married man with one child, a daughter named Colombe, about the same age as Charles, the younger of the Sanson boys.

Pierre Brossier treated these two nephews as he did his own daughter, bringing them up as one family. He decided that Jean-Baptiste should study for the law; meanwhile, the two much younger children played together like brother and sister. By the time they reached their majority, Jean-Baptiste was a counsellor at Abbeville law-courts; his uncle had recently bought him this office.

The story up to that point is authentic. But no document exists to support the account of the tragedy of Charles Sanson the First described by the last of the Sansons; so it must be accepted with reserve. This episode occupies half of one of the six volumes of the 'Memoirs'. Put briefly, and eliminating all the extravagances making it an old-fashioned melodrama, the account is as follows:

Charles Sanson and Colombe Brossier were then in their twenties; while Jean-Baptiste was over thirty and, to the satisfaction of his uncle, had recently qualified for the law.

The kindred feelings between Charles and Colombe had developed into more tender sentiments. They had avowed their love to each other and, while remaining as chaste as their passion was pure, were awaiting a favourable opportunity for asking Pierre Brossier to agree to their marriage. This idyll had escaped the notice of the seigneur de Limeux, and of Charles's brother too. Was there still a Madame Brossier de Limeux, the mother who could have seen into her daughter's heart? The story does not say.

One day, believing he was acting like a good father, Pierre Brossier told Colombe in the presence of her two cousins: 'My dear child, Jean-Baptiste is about to begin his functions at the law-courts. This honorific and lucrative office calls for a wife in the home. It's needless to look very far for her — I announce your engagement to him.'

The poor girl and her lover were struck all of a heap. That evening, however, they both told the father of their love for each other. He laughed at them, but when the young couple persisted his amusement turned to anger. For him, love had no place in marriage; that was a serious business not to be hindered by frivolous sentiments. Jean-Baptiste was a magistrate, Charles was still a mere youngster — what comparison was possible between them? Besides, the rights of seniority prevailed. So there it was — Colombe would marry Jean-Baptiste.

'At your age,' Charles's uncle said to him in conclusion, 'a younger son thinks of serving the King and not of enriching himself by taking a wife.'

Enriching himself! As though the unfortunate young man fostered such a base design . . .

In short, having persisted for over an hour and realised that nothing would shake Colombe's father, Charles left him and the hapless girl, who had collapsed in tears and was incapable of holding Charles back. Then, without a farewell to his brother, who was absent, Charles left the house and took the road to Paris.

Soon after reaching the capital he joined the musketeers, and spent the next three years serving his King in the province of Quebec, which Champlain had founded in 1608. Charles first faced fire in a skirmish against colonists in revolt against the royal authority. He was in fights against the Indians, and followed the custom of the times by augmenting his pay with loot. The gold and precious stones he accumulated gave him the impression of being rich. He forgot about Colombe in the arms of several dusky squaws.

Not entirely, though, for he and Colombe wrote to each other. The letters were few and far between, naturally, but he learnt of her marriage to his brother and their early life together, a life not of their choosing and apparently uneventful.

At the end of three years Charles returned to France, landing at Toulon. A letter from his sister-in-law, who knew he was returning, awaited him there. It begged him to go to her at once. Colombe gave no details and did not mention Jean-Baptiste. Fearing some disaster, Charles obtained leave of absence, got himself a horse and set off.

A fortnight after leaving Toulon the weary traveller saw the towers of Abbeville church in the distance. As he rode through the narrow streets of his native town and saw once again the old, overhanging houses with their carved beam-ends he felt a lump come to his throat. He hurried along to the Place Saint-Jean and dismounted in front of his uncle's house. The high-pitched roof, the narrow, pointed windows and the brown-and-white half-timbered walls reminded him of his childhood, his youth, and his love for Colombe. With some trepidation, he raised the knocker. He banged again, but still no one came to the door. A neighbour put his head out of a window and, recognising Charles, told him that Counsellor Sanson de Longval had moved out to the Faubourg d'Amiens a year ago.

'And the Sieur Brossier de Limeux?' asked Charles.

'He's dead,' the other replied.

Charles mounted his horse again, and a few minutes later was knocking at a house in the suburbs pointed out to him by a local woman. It was a humble abode, giving even an impression of poverty. A woman called 'Come in'. He recognised Colombe's voice, and a tremor went through him.

As he pushed at the door it opened before him and a woman fell into his arms. The two stayed closely locked for some moments, not uttering a word. Then, recovering herself, Colombe stepped back blushing with shame. To cover this momentary weakness she addressed him as 'brother', to which he replied with 'little sister'. She took him by the hand and, seeming to take no notice of his more mature air, his bronzed face and thin moustache, led him into a room where a man was dozing in an armchair. His face was horribly marked by cuts and grooves, with the skin all puckered, reminding Charles of the tattooed Indians he had seen in America. Hearing the couple step into the room, the man raised his head and turned blank eyes towards them; and Charles saw that it was his brother and that he was blind.

The traveller looked aghast from Jean-Baptiste to Colombe, who was silently weeping. Forcing back his own tears, Charles went and embraced his brother, forgetting all his old grudges. When all three had recovered from their emotion, the mutilated man himself told Charles of his misfortunes.

Their uncle had died two years previously, leaving his fief of Limeux to Colombe. But the overlord had at once withdrawn the concession. Jean-Baptiste took the matter to court, believing that his office of counsellor would facilitate his victory. Unfortunately for him, his uncle's title-deeds were not in order. Jean-Baptiste had pleaded his case, but in vain. He not only lost the revenues from Limeux, but had to sell the house in the Place Saint-Jean to pay the costs of the lawsuit. And, as troubles never come singly, a linen-merchant he had guaranteed went bankrupt and Jean-Baptiste had been obliged to part with his own fief, that of Longval, to help pay the creditors.

Crushed by this double misfortune, he had fallen ill. Left alone one day when Colombe had gone to market, he was suddenly seized by a kind of epileptic fit and fell head foremost into the fire on the hearth, losing consciousness. When his wife returned she had found him paralysed, his face burnt, and blinded.

Unable to work, he had had to sell his office of counsellor. Since then, the couple had lived on the small income from the amount received.

After hearing all this, there was no longer any question of Charles returning to sea! He placed the wealth that his service in Canada had brought him at his brother's disposal. 'We'll all live together,' he declared, renouncing his career as a soldier. 'There'll be two of us to look after you.'

The age of the invalid was then thirty-five, his wife and his brother were twenty-four.

Neither Pierre Brossier nor his daughter had told Jean-Baptiste the real cause of Charles leaving home. The counsellor had guessed nevertheless, but to him it was just one of those childish things that men of upright yet cold heart see in true love. Now that he was impotent, did he feel uneasy about his brother and Colombe being in the same house again? Or did he resign himself to what might happen, ready to sacrifice his honour for his material peace of mind? In any case, fearing that his brother on whom he was financially dependent might become bored after leading such an adventurous life abroad, Jean-Baptiste persuaded his wife to 'do all she could to prevent Charles becoming dissatisfied and leaving them.' Colombe, however, — added the writer of the 'Memoirs' — 'was chaste enough to have no suspicion of the danger she was exposing herself to.'

Did the inevitable occur? Apparently not, for Charles went away again after a time; though not without having tried to persuade the over-faithful wife in name only to yield to him. One evening he took her ready lips, and would have taken the rest too if Colombe, recovering herself, had not exclaimed: 'God has ordained we shall never be more than brother and sister! Let us respect His will, and not sigh with regret for the dreams of our youth! I can still love you without it being a crime.'

And the idyll stayed at that.

At first reading, this story seems plausible. On reflection, it appears less so. And this is given some support by the remainder of the story. Charles loved his brother and adored his sister-in-law. If he wanted to help them financially and also to flee from the dangers of a love revived, he could have left the hoard from Canada with them and gone overseas again to carve out a fresh fortune. Yet he did not rejoin his ship at Toulon. Instead — so his descendant tells us — 'desiring to watch over the dear ones whose only support he was,' he purchased a lieutenancy in the Regiment de la Boissière, which was in garrison at Dieppe.

In those times anyone with pretence to gentle birth could buy a commission. According to his means, he obtained command of a platoon, a company, or even a regiment — which then took the name of its new owner. Thus had the regiment quartered at Dieppe in 1661 been named after the Marquis de la Boissière. Charles Sanson had heard there was a lieutenancy in it for sale, and so had gone to live about forty miles away from his brother and Colombe.

She and Charles had no communication with each other at first. But she knew where he was, for on May 31st, 1662, she sent him a new appeal for financial help, adding that Jean-Baptiste was getting worse every day. Charles sent some money, but did not go to see them.

Months passed, a few more letters were exchanged . . .

One summer's afternoon Charles rode down from Dieppe castle, where the regiment was quartered, to find a messenger waiting outside his lodging with a letter for him. The lieutenant recognised Colombe's writing and opened it at once. His face went grave; Jean-Baptiste was dead. Moreover, creditors had seized the house and contents, after the funeral, and the widow had been put out on the street. She had thought of her brother-in-law and had set out on foot to reach him, and had managed to get three-quarters of the way. Then, completely exhausted, she had stopped at a farm near Envermeu, a village about four leagues from Dieppe. She was there now, awaiting Charles, hoping he would come and conduct her to a convent where she would end her days.

Charles dismissed the messenger, mounted his horse and galloped off in the direction of Envermeu. Night was falling when he arrived; on the steps of the market-cross a small dark shape was stretched out. He stopped and dismounted, recognised Colombe, and made to take her in his arms. Instead of accepting this invitation, Colombe turned and pointed to the cross. Charles then merely helped her to her feet, calling her 'little sister' as in the past.

Side by side, they went to the farmhouse where the bereaved young woman had spent the previous night. On the way, she told him about the death of Jean-Baptiste and the heartlessness of the creditors who had seized the house. He paid the peasants for Colombe's night's lodging, and then put her astride his horse. Taking the bridle, he began to walk back towards Dieppe.

An hour later the couple were passing along some cliffs overlooking the Channel. The sun had disappeared into the sea, but its last dying embers were draped around heavy black clouds gathering at the end of this stifling summer's day. The atmosphere became heavy and close. In a matter of minutes the whole sky was covered by a sheet of inky darkness, and large drops of rain began to spatter the ground. The shower soon became a downpour, and then a deluge. Lightning flashed and thunder roared, crackling and echoing all around with frightening effect.

'Mount with me and gallop away!' cried Colombe.

Charles did so, one arm clasped round the young woman's waist, and gripping the reins with the other hand. The storm increased in intensity; all hell seemed let loose. The horse, terrified by the thunder and lightning and torrential rain, raced madly along without needing to be spurred. In her fright, Colombe clung tightly to Charles, and he held her closely to him as they sped like phantoms through the darkness lit here and there by streaks of lightning. The lieutenant's passion for Colombe rose anew, and he pressed his ardent lips against her brow.

Suddenly, a ball of fire crashed down just in front of their steed. The animal stopped dead, and the two riders were hurled forward over its head.

When Charles regained consciousness he found himself in bed in a sunny room. He was aware of an unknown girl bending over him and smiling. He tried to speak, but only unintelligible sounds came forth; then his senses left him again.

For some days he remained in a state halfway between sleep and a hazy awareness of his surroundings. Three persons succeeded each other at his bedside: the girl with the smile of a Madonna, an old woman who rebuked her sharply while appearing to obey her, and a man in his fifties, heavily bearded and with the build of a giant. He would order the two women from the room and then tend Charles as a doctor might have done.

As soon as he was able to speak, the sick man asked for Colombe. At that moment only the girl was watching over him. She did not seem to understand, though he repeated the beloved name several times. Then, making a great effort, he added 'my sister'. Tears came into the eyes fixed on him; the girl crossed herself. Charles, realising the terrible truth, fell back in a faint.

A day came when Charles was able to thank his host and hear what had happened. His saviours had found the two riders lying in the road; the horse had made off, Colombe was dead, but Charles was still breathing. Some monks fetched from Dieppe had taken the dead woman and buried her in the town's cemetery, while the man and his servant had carried Charles to their house, which was close to the scene of the accident and was called *Le Clos Mauduit* — The Accursed Enclosure.

Charles wept for his sister-in-law, but in spite of this sorrow he gradually got better. The girl no longer came to see him. This surprised him, as did the refusal of his host to say anything about himself.

'Who are you?' Charles asked the man who had saved his life.

'My name would mean nothing to you,' the other replied. 'If you think you owe me some thanks, you can show it by not insisting.'

'Before I leave your house could I at least see the kind girl again — whom I take to be your daughter — to thank her for looking after me and say farewell?'

'No, you can't.'

This double refusal, coming so harshly after all the kindness received, disturbed the convalescent. He began to think these people were suspicious of him, that the father feared he had designs on the daughter of the house. No sooner had the idea entered his head than it troubled him. The more he tried to overcome the desire, which seemed an offence to Colombe's memory, the stronger it became. He could hold out no longer, and repeated his request to the father.

Suppressing his anger, the latter replied: 'Sir, you are almost well again. A journey of one league will not tire you, if transport is provided. My servant is taking a waggon to Dieppe tonight. He will put you down at your lodgings. Tomorrow, if you wish, you will be able to find out where your sister is buried, from the keeper of the cemetery.'

Somewhat surprised, Charles merely murmured his thanks. He got up and dressed himself that evening, but stayed in his room until the master of the *Clos Mauduit* came to fetch him. Night had fallen; a waggon and its driver were waiting in the courtyard. Just before leaving, Charles noticed a curtain drawn timidly aside and the girl's face appeared, lit by a candle and exceedingly sad.

The horse broke into a trot. On the way, the lieutenant tried to engage the driver in conversation; but the latter, a big, stoutly-built fellow, met every question with a grunt. Was this rustic dumb, Charles wondered? In the darkness he could just discern what the waggon was carrying — an iron brasier, some lengths of metal, an iron club, long pincers, rope, and a wheel placed flat and slowly turning on its hub. It seemed an extraordinary collection.

Back in Dieppe, he presented himself before the Marquis de la Boissière and explained the reasons for his long absence. With time, he completely recovered from his accident; only his heart remained affected, sorrowing over the tragic end of Colombe and trying to forget his pretty nurse at the *Clos Mauduit*. He was astonished by this transfer of his feelings; the remembrance and image of the living girl continually clouded over those of the dead woman. He rebuked himself for it, but all to no use. He knew little about the girl except her name: Marguerite — that was how her father and the old governess had addressed her, Charles could just recall. And did that unreasonable father have such a shameful calling as to be obliged to remain stubbornly silent about himself?

Day after day, Charles thus suffered distress and anguish. But after some weeks he began to find pleasure in life again, and the passage of time healed the wounds in his heart left by Colombe and effaced the memory of Marguerite.

However, when on manœuvres with his regiment he found himself in the neighbourhood of the *Clos Mauduit*. Seeing the roof of the house in the distance, he could contain himself no longer, and galloped towards it. Through the hedge he caught sight of the girl watering flowers in the garden. She was alone; being near her revived his passion. Jumping the hedge, he ran towards her and exclaimed, 'Your crusty old father prevented me from thanking you, so I've come to express my gratitude for your kind, charitable services!'

Then, without any transition, he declared his love for her. She coloured, and turned her head away. He edged round her, and saw tears in her eyes.

'Why are you crying?' he asked.

She hesitated a moment, then replied, 'You mustn't fall in love with me. It would bring great trouble on your head. Go right away, my father might come. Never speak to me again.' And she fled into the house, forcing back her sobs.

Charles returned to Dieppe bewildered and frustrated. Some

mystery was obviously hidden behind the walls of the *Clos Mauduit*. He could not rest content until he had discovered what it was. During the days following he went back and roamed around the house which was so hospitable to the injured yet so barred to the hale and hearty. Marguerite's tears had proved to him that she shared his love. He watched out for her from a distance; and, catching sight of her on one occasion, made signs to her. She seemed about to reply, then suddenly changed her mind. Turning on her heels, she disappeared.

He ended by convincing himself that he was confusing love with desire, and thought he might thereby exorcise his burning passion. At first he rejected the idea, but it returned and gained ground. After all, ravishing a virgin was a common enough occurrence among great lords — the example was set from above! So, as an abscess is pricked to put an end to the suffering, Charles Sanson de Longval decided to possess Marguerite, come what may.

How did he manage to fulfil his wicked intention? The account in the 'novel' compiled by d'Olbreuse and the last of the Sansons cannot be accepted. Although the manners of the times were rough and lewd, it is impossible to believe that Charles and two other officers resolved to ravish the girl while she was in a deep sleep, and to that end gave a narcotic to the father's servant for him to put into the family's drinks!

All the same, Charles Sanson made Marguerite his mistress. The first occasion they made love together was in the girl's bedroom, with the complicity of the governess, one night when her father and his servant were both absent from the house. What were they doing in Dieppe? At this point the real drama begins. The triumphant lover was returning to his lodgings, humming over his conquest as his horse trotted along, and still enraptured by his minutes in the virginal bed, when, reaching Dieppe and crossing the Place du Puits-Salé as dawn was breaking, he saw the public executioner of the province putting some criminals into a pillory set up on a platform. This gruesome expert, Charles recognised with horror, was none other than Marguerite's father! Pierre Jouenne, the appointed executioner for Rouen, Caudebec-

en-Caux, and the viscounty of Dieppe, was carrying out one of
his functions — standing malefactors in the pillory.

The lieutenant almost collapsed. A common hangman — his
mistress's father was the common hangman! The name of Pierre
Jouenne was well known to Charles, as to everybody in Dieppe.
But Charles had never before seen him carrying out his functions.

For some weeks Charles managed to keep a check on himself,
and stayed away from the *Clos Mauduit*. But finally, unable to
contain his rage and passion, he set off to see his dear mistress
and ask her for an explanation. Marguerite ought to have told
him the truth! Does a girl let herself be seduced by a man of
gentle birth (or claiming to be) when she is the daughter of a
public executioner?

What took place between them? The story is silent over this,
but reveals that the lovers subsequently met on several occasions,
in tender circumstances and at night, when Pierre Jouenne was
away performing his sinister functions at Rouen, Yvetot, or
elsewhere. Before long, their fiery passion passed all restraint.
Neglecting the simplest precautions, Charles went to Marguerite
in full daylight. In the country, nothing is secret for long; and
one morning the Marquis de la Boissière sent for Charles Sanson.

'I hear odd reports about you,' said the Marquis. 'You are
bringing dishonour upon my regiment. You are having a dis-
graceful love affair with a harlot, the public executioner's
daughter! Consider yourself confined to barracks. I shall write to
the King — he will decide whether you are to be dismissed the
regiment.'

Furious at the colonel's insulting references to Marguerite,
Charles drew his sword and broke it across his knee.

'There's no need to write to the King!' he retorted. 'I resign my
commission, and I'm going back to my billet to tear it up!'

He went to his room, gathered up some money, mounted his
horse and galloped off to the *Clos Mauduit*.

He found the father, daughter, and the governess in the middle
of a quarrel. Pierre Jouenne had heard the rumours about
Marguerite, and knew she had a lover. Sword in hand, he was
threatening to kill her if she did not divulge the name of her

seducer. Charles arrived opportunely. Declaring himself, he offered to marry Marguerite and to take her with him to Canada.

The girl agreed to the marriage but refused to leave her father.

'Then let him come with us!' exclaimed Sanson.

Pierre Jouenne shook his head. There would be no question of him performing his grisly functions in America. That was all very well, but would not prevent his son-in-law from despising him, and incidentally Marguerite. And if Charles went off, the poor girl would no longer be able to find a husband. Only another executioner married the daughter of one, a person inevitably considered an outcast; and therefore expected the one advantage possible — for his fiancée to be a virgin. Charles had seduced Marguerite; he must do the honourable thing and marry her, and then follow his father-in-law's occupation and eventually succeed him.

'Take it or leave it,' concluded Pierre Jouenne. 'But if you refuse, I'll kill Marguerite.'

We are not told whether the lieutenant agreed at once. But it would appear that he did in the end, for the official report of an execution carried out at Rouen contains these words:

'Having to break a certain Martin Eslau on the wheel, and Maistre Pierre Jouenne, the public executioner, having forced his son-in-law, recently married, to hit at the condemned man with an iron bar, the said son-in-law fell in a swoon and was jeered at by the crowd.'

CHAPTER TWO

Charles 1, the pitiful

CHARLES SANSON served as assistant to his father-in-law for some years. The old maxim, 'As insolent as an executioner's assistant', could hardly be applied to him, for his sad face and humble, polite ways were the mark of his shame. He had accepted his horrible fate, and forgot his stigma in the arms of Marguerite.

He only served as an underling when on the scaffold with the public executioner. Unlike other executioners' assistants, he did not do household chores nor wait at table. Being the son-in-law, he did not have to exchange his stained leather apron for a livery on returning to the house.

His wife's family and the members of the confraternity nevertheless gave him a nickname, following a curious tradition. Whether servants were the aides to public executioners or belonged to some grand household, their masters called them by the name of their home-town more often than by their proper name. 'Saint-Germain, go and tell Bordeaux to get out my carriage, and tell Villers-Cotterêts that he's to drive,' appears in a manuscript of the times. Charles Sanson, though, was not called 'Abbeville' (which would seem logical) but 'Longval' — which recognised his pretensions to the seigniory of the small Picardy fief. He was called Longval by his wife's family, all of whose menfolk had the same occupation as Pierre Jouenne. The Jouennes appear in the records as public executioners right up to the end of the 18th century. They all carried out their functions in the provinces, not one gaining promotion to Paris. Hanging people or breaking them on the wheel in the capital gave a singular esteem, to which considerable revenues were attached. All the Jouennes, uncles or cousins of Marguerite, hoped to get the rich Paris appointment, but none ever did. To become the executioner of Parisians, the office had to be vacant, the applicant had to be able to pay heavily for it, and the King himself had to approve the new slayer. Three conditions difficult to fulfil at one time.

Now in 1687 the Paris executioner was relieved of his office for some venial fault. His name was Nicolas Levasseur, called La Rivière, and although there is no proof it would seem that the reason for his dismissal was a tax he levied on the women of the town. The executioner at Orléans was authorised to do this, and his Paris counterpart believed he was too. He was married to a Jouenne, a cousin of Marguerite with the same name, and so all the Jouenne family knew of the vacancy.

Charles Sanson had succeeded to his father-in-law's place several years previously. His previous fears were now forgotten; he did his work without flagging or dreading it.

Nicolas Levasseur, although dismissed, was allowed to sell his office. He asked a high price for it, in view of the revenues and advantages that went with it. None of the Jouennes had enough money, but Sanson apparently had, as it was he who succeeded Levasseur. His 'letters of appointment' — which still exist in the Archives Nationales — are dated September 23rd, 1688. The opening words are:

'Louis, par la grâce de Dieu roy de France et de Navarre, à tous ceux qui ces présentes verront, salut.' And continues — 'By ordinance of our Court of Parlement of Paris, the 11th of August of the present year, it having been directed for reasons following that Charles Sanson, called Longval, will alone act as public executioner in our city and jurisdiction of Paris, provided he obtains our letters of appointment to the said office. Be it known that, for the good report made to us on the person of the aforesaid Charles Sanson, called Longval, we have, in conformity with the said decision, given and granted to him, and do give and grant to him by these presents the office of executioner of capital and criminal sentences in our aforesaid city, jurisdiction, and viscounty of Paris...'

This warrant, which cost Sanson 6,000 livres for its frais de chauffecire — for being sealed and registered — enumerated the advantages granted to the holder after he had taken the oath of office. They represented an unusual manner of receiving pay. The public executioner was given no salary, but was allowed a levy in cash or kind on various categories of traders. This levy, or tax, was called the *droit de havage* or *droit de havée*. (From *havir*, which means 'to scorch', but which in the past also meant 'to dip into'.)

The goods and receipts that the public executioner could 'dip into' were quite numerous. Among the market traders at Les Halles he could take an egg from each basket, a fruit or a bunch of grapes from each crate, a small or large fish from each barrel, a handful of vegetables from each crate put on sale; he levied a *sou* for each barrow unloaded, two *sous* for a one-horse cart, twice that amount for a cart and pair, and so on.

The public executioner did not in fact 'dip in' with his hands, but with a spoon — the change had taken place in the previous century, when the traders had protested against the contact of such a bloodstained fist. Moreover, the executioner no longer went round the market in person; he delegated his assistants, each having an area for 'dipping his spoon' into crates, baskets, and satchels.

No regulation or order limited the number of assistants, so the beneficiary used the pretext of numerous executions to employ many and thus increase the levy. The expression 'as insolent as an executioner's assistant' derives from this practice; the toughs collected these dues with a disdain that hardly accorded with their social position, and had no hesitation about claiming perquisites for themselves.

The public executioner thus received enormous quantities of foodstuffs, and their sale left him comfortably off. He collected this levy not only from traders at the central market but also at the gates of Paris, on all food being carted directly to the shops. His assistants there 'dipped in their spoons' to the same effect. But when a cart carrying coal came by, the executioner's agent could 'fill his stock-pot' — as Sanson's letters of appointment put it.

In addition, he was exempted from paying tolls at fords, bridges, and footways, and dues on wine and other drinks brought in for his own use; and also had the right to carry offensive and defensive arms for himself and his servants because of his office.

In short, by paying no taxes and receiving dues in cash and in kind, the public executioner obtained an annual revenue of between forty and sixty thousand *livres*. These approximate figures — which were mentioned in the Parlement when the *droit de havage* was abolished — took into account the professional expenses of the executioner, the keep and pay of his menials and the fodder for his horses. Everything else, the ropes and the whips, the axes and swords, were provided free by the various guilds. He was supposed to have as many assistants as there were different food pavilions at the Halles and gates to Paris. In fact, some people were envious of the sanguinary official; 'as rich as the hangman' was an expression often heard in 17th-century France.

As lodgings for his family and servants, and to store his merchandise and his necessary instruments, Sanson had the use — again quoting from his letters of appointment — 'of the house by the Pillory of the Halles, its sheds and outbuildings, and is not to be troubled or disturbed there for any cause whatever.'

This pillory was actually a one-storied octagonal tower, the upper part — on which was the pillory proper — made to rotate on the lower. Every so often, one of Sanson's assistants gave a push and sent the upper half turning so that the men and women in the pillory were shown to everyone standing round. Each of these offenders bore a notice — 'swindler', 'fraud', 'bigamist', 'brothel-keeper', 'bankrupt', or 'blashphemer'. A constable stood on guard at the foot of the tower to stop onlookers from throwing muck or water — though not ribald remarks — at the helpless victims. It was usual for criminals sentenced to the galleys, to be banished, or to a term of imprisonment, to be put in the pillory for six hours before being taken away to begin their sentence.

The public executioner's house adjoined the pillory-tower, though the latter rose high above it. They stood behind the church of St. Eustache, in the middle of a square that is today the place where the rue Montmartre, the rue Montorgueil, and the rue

Turbigo meet, opposite the main entrance to Les Halles. The public executioner thus lived in the centre of the busiest and noisiest district of Paris. None of his comings and goings, nor any of his activities, escaped the notice of the numerous traders and their throng of regular customers. And Heaven knows he was far from idle! Apart from seeing that the shameful punishment of standing people in the pillory was carried out, he went daily to the Hôtel de Ville to supervise the executions that took place in the square in front. 'There are usually two or three condemned prisoners hanged or broken on the wheel every day, except fête-days,' impassively wrote a priest from Bologna, Sebastiano Locatelli, who spent a winter in Paris during the reign of Louis XIV. And he did not mention the beheadings, the whippings, the brandings, nor the people burnt at the stake! In short, Charles Sanson had to do plenty for the fifty or sixty thousand *livres* he received each year.

For Marguerite, after the quiet countryside and the remoteness of the *Clos Mauduit*, what a change it was to be living in the centre of Paris, and to hear people mutter as she went by, 'That's the wife of the hangman.' Did she think the great improvement in their income was sufficient compensation? It is hardly likely. The young woman found living in a thickly-populated district a great trial; she disliked the comings and goings of the assistants, was sickened by the noises from the shed where the instruments of punishment were kept, by the lamentations from the pillory and the insults shouted at the prisoners, and she was made miserable by the change in her husband's character, for he had become gloomy and taciturn.

To make things worse, they always had one or two corpses on their hands. If the bodies of executed prisoners were not claimed by their families, Sanson was obliged to take them home until the clergy decided where to bury them. A small outhouse, between the stable and the coach-house, did duty as a mortuary. In summer, awful smells often came from it. Marguerite, who had been able to forget her father's sinister occupation in the sweet rustic surroundings of the *Clos Mauduit*, found the house by the pillory to be a purgatory, almost a hell on earth.

She and Charles had a son who was seven when they first settled in Paris, in 1688, and who had been named after his father. The young Charles grew up amid all the horrors of the establishment. There were no playmates for him, except the children of his father's assistants; no going to school, where he could have breathed something of the freshness of youth and mixed with the offspring of respectable burgesses. Who wants to play with a son of the public executioner? A good-hearted priest came to the Pillory house every day; after briefly greeting Madame Sanson, he taught the poor boy reading and writing, some arithmetic and history, and the catechism. Sometimes he took young Charles out for a walk. How difficult it must have been to find something to talk about! The everlasting 'why' and 'what' of children always came back to the same problem...

Through dealing out death, Sanson began to want to find out its secrets. To be able to ease people's pains and sufferings seemed to him a way of redemption, a kind of moral and secular absolution. Although the dissecting of human bodies was no longer counted a crime, it was nevertheless still regarded as smacking of the devil. Certain men of learning, however, were allowed to practise it, to the detriment of others. Fontenelle, speaking at the Académie des Sciences, protested against this arbitrariness, and added: 'One is reduced to getting round the law and to gaining knowledge by pilferings that are always rather risky.'

Charles Sanson could forgo these pilferings. He had no need to rely on body-snatchers, for there was always a corpse or two in one of his outhouses. One night when all the household was asleep he slipped in there, and uncovered a body which his assistants had cut off from life that very morning. Bravely starting on his self-imposed task, Charles slid his knife into the cold, inert flesh. Beads of sweat glistened on his brow. A candle stuck in the wall threw a flickering light on the muscles and sinews that he uncovered. As he worked, forcing back his fears, he had the appearance of some sadistic, dangerous madman. The creaking of the weathervane on top of the pillory-tower gave an appropriate sound-effect to the dreadful task. Although horrified by what he was doing, Sanson went through with it. Patiently and methodically, though now and again almost giving up, the man who dealt out death was seeking the secret of life.

Some days later he began again on another victim; and so, by repeating his dissections over a period of many months, Sanson eventually acquired an extensive knowledge of the human anatomy. He bought the few medical and surgical books available, and compared his discoveries with their findings. Some curious connections he noticed between the play of certain muscles and their articulations led him to think of and make up ointments for easing particular pains. He tried them out on himself, his family and servants, and gradually obtained a reputation as a healer within the circle of law-officers, which drew him a few clients. The news got around and his public widened. Later, his son and descendants continued and improved the remedies. In the 18th century the 'executioner's balsam' had the reputation more or less justified of easing the most persistent rheumatism. Other remedies issued from the Sanson dispensary, and the last of the line wrote (though his words cannot be confirmed): 'We sold these remedies at a high price, I admit, to the aristocracy and rich people; but we gave them without charge to the poor. That compensated for it.'

The Pillory house was State property, in other words the King's. The occupier paid no rent, but he received some from the eight or ten wooden shops abutting on the walls. These shops provided an additional income but increased the noise in the immediate neighbourhood; Marguerite's health suffered from it, and so did her son's education.

The shopkeepers began setting out their goods soon after dawn every morning, arguing with their wives and scolding their apprentices. The noises grew as the shoppers arrived, and the confusion of sounds from the main market added to the tumult. By the middle of the morning there was a constant din all round the house.

Before convicted bankrupts were put in the pillory they had to express remorse for their misdeeds at the foot of a stone cross, just in front of the Pillory house. Crowds quickly gathered as soon as they were put into the pillory; and never a day passed without a number of malefactors being exposed to view. When a bigamist was brought along by the constables, an ignominious whipping was administered first — whatever the person's sex. Prostitutes convicted of making a public nuisance received similar punishment. These whippings always drew a great throng of people. When the uproar was at its height, when the screams of the women as the whip fell on their bare backs were being greeted by lewd comment and ironic jeers from the crowd, it often happened that the door of the outhouse where Sanson kept his material opened and a horse and cart came out carrying the public executioner and some of his assistants, on their way to the Châtelet to collect a prisoner sentenced to death and then to take him to the Place de Grève for the execution. On these occasions Sanson wore his uniform in the city's colours, a red jacket and blue breeches; a gibbet was embroidered in black on the front of the jacket, and a ladder on the back. When Sanson appeared, the uproar died down and the crowd made way for his cart; to impede the executioner was considered an offence against the law and its officers. But the tumult rose again as soon as the Sword of Justice had disappeared from view.

Meanwhile, arguments would be constantly breaking out between the tradespeople in the Halles and the 'holders of the spoon'. These peculiar tax-gatherers, sure of their rights and the support of the authorities, were not content with just dipping in their spoons; and their greed and arrogance led to disputes that sometimes ended in fights.

All this terrible noise assailed Marguerite and almost drove her mad. It made her anxious for young Charles too, whose education and upbringing suffered from the daily sights and sounds around him. Matters reached such a point that Charles Sanson, worried about the health of his wife and son, decided to move to a quieter district; for the conditions of his appointment did not oblige him to live at the Pillory house. He settled on an area about a mile to the north, what is now the Faubourg Poissonnière. In Sanson's time it was mainly fields, with a few farmhouses, and contained

the convent of St. Lazare, and two churches, St. Anne's and
St. Laurent's.

Sanson bought a house near St. Anne's church (now destroyed).
There was a garden round it, outbuildings where his assistants
could sleep, and where he could stable his horses and carts and
store his instruments of punishment and death.

He found a tenant for the Pillory house, at a rental of 600 *livres*
a year, and only went back there to preside at some notable
pillorying, which was carried out by his assistants. On such
occasions he put on his red and blue uniform. When not
appearing in his official capacity, he dressed like a middleclass
merchant and wore a sword like a nobleman, which his appointment permitted him to do. Besides, he still maintained his claim
to the seigniory of Longval.

In spite of the move to cleaner air and away from the sights and
sounds of punishment being inflicted, Marguerite's health
continued to deteriorate. The day came when she had to take to
her bed, never to rise from it again. The nature of her illness is
not known, nor the date of her death.

In his book, *The Guillotine during the Revolution*, Georges
Lenotre wrote at some length about the ancestors of the Sanson
who executed Louis XVI, and stated, 'Marguerite Jouenne died
young.' The well-known historian of the Revolution was no
doubt satisfied to rely on the words of the last of the Sansons:
'It was at the end of 1685 that my ancestor, Charles Sanson de
Longval, left Normandy and the last resting-place of this
Marguerite Jouanne *(sic)* who had brought him such a dowry of
horror.'

But there are two errors in that statement. In the first place,
Sanson went to take up his Paris office in 1688 (as his letters of
appointment prove); and secondly, his wife Marguerite was
buried in the church of St. Laurent, in Paris. In 1688, the ex-
lieutenant was 53. At the time of the idyll at the *Clos Mauduit*
he had just reached his thirties, Marguerite being about ten years
younger. Their son was born in 1681, and in Normandy, when
Marguerite must have been quite 35; and when she died in Paris,
this son was already an assistant to his father.

Whatever the date of her death, Charles soon found loneliness a burden too heavy to bear and eventually married again. In 1699, the year of his second marriage, he was 64; prematurely aged by the trials and sorrows in his youth and by his experiences in later life, he was a broken man and the slightest noise made him start. In his silent, lonely hours he recalled not only the images of the two women in his life but also the spectres of those many other women whom, over the years, he had conducted to their sudden end. There seems no doubt he had been very susceptible to feminine charms and ready for love; it was that which had caused him to accept becoming a social outcast. So one can understand his mental sufferings each time the guilty person to be executed was a woman whose youth or beauty pleaded for her.

Among the women victims who most obsessed his memory were those who had struggled with the fury of despair and those who, on the contrary, had accepted their fate with meekness and feminine grace. And one of the latter, Madame Tiquet, was very fresh in his mind. It was that experience which set him yearning more than ever for a second wife, for a companion able to bring balm to his sufferings.

This Madame Tiquet had been the wife of a counsellor at the Paris Parlement. She greatly reminded Charles of his poor Colombe, wife of a counsellor at the Abbeville Courts; both had been of the same height, had the same colour of hair, a similar appearance and, to complete it all, had an unfortunate marriage. But whereas Colombe had accepted the upright Jean-Baptiste with good grace and fulfilled her wifely duties, Angélique Tiquet had rebelled against the meanness, the brutality and conceit, and the infidelities of her husband. Unable to stand it any longer, she had in turn been unfaithful to him, and then plotted to have him assassinated. But at the last moment, perhaps through remorse or fear of discovery, she called off the thugs she had paid to kill the counsellor in a little-frequented street. Nevertheless the plot was denounced, she was arrested, convicted of a capital offence and sentenced to death, although her husband begged for her life to be spared.

The day following the verdict a great crowd gathered in the

Place de Grève to see the execution. Paris was sweltering in a heat-wave; thunderstorms were threatening, reminding the ex-lieutenant of another storm and another counsellor's wife who had died while the lightning flashed and the thunder roared. The executioner's cart advanced through the crowd at a walking-pace, drawn by a pair of horses and escorted by soldiers. Angélique, her hair hanging down over the white gown of a condemned woman, seemed reconciled to her fate. She was sitting on a wooden form listening to her confessor, the *abbé* de la Chétârdie, who was exhorting her to be brave; but she had no lack of courage. Charles, standing beside her in his red and blue uniform, could not help thinking of Colombe as he saw the sky darkening.

Just as the cart arrived in front of the Hôtel de Ville, the first streak of lightning flashed across the sky; a clap of thunder quickly followed, and then the rain fell in torrents. Everyone ran for shelter, under porches, under balconies and shop awnings; the executioner's assistants huddled beneath the scaffold, the soldiers beneath the cart. Only Sanson, Angélique, and the priest, remained where they were, getting soaked to the skin.

'Please forgive me for making you wait until the storm is over,' Charles said to the woman. 'But a downpour like this might cause the sword to slip; you'd risk suffering unnecessarily.'

For condemned prisoners of rank did not die under the axe, a weapon of common people, but were despatched by the sword, a noble arm. The sword used by the public executioner was a long, double-bladed weapon, and so heavy that both hands were needed. If not expertly aimed it might fall on the head or shoulder instead of the neck, and Sanson feared that the crash of thunder and the lightning and heavy rain might cause the sword to deviate — after swinging it round three times to get enough force to cut clean through the neck.

Madame Tiquet thanked the aged man for his solicitude and, still calm, waited for the storm to pass. This dismal situation lasted an hour. The rain streamed down the poor woman; her long loose hair became plastered to her head and the white gown stuck to her body, revealing the splendours of her figure. Charles, seeing her there so slim and gracious and resigned, thought even more of Colombe and the storm that had caused her death; and he started to tremble and shake.

The rain began to stop at last. The crowd gradually gathered in the square again, Sanson's assistants and the soldiers emerged from their shelters. A rumour went round that Louis XIV had pardoned the condemned woman. Sanson, standing in the cart, kept glancing round hoping to see a horseman come through the crowd with a message that would keep the executioner's sword in its scabbard. After waiting in vain for several minutes, Charles had to force himself to carry on. He put a hand on Angélique's shoulder. 'The moment has come,' he said with shammed roughness, mainly to bolster up his own courage. But he added, 'You must forgive me, Madame.'

She stepped down from the cart and walked towards the scaffold on the arm of the priest holding his crucifix, her bare feet splashing through the puddles. When she had climbed the steps, preceded by Sanson, she asked him to give her his hand. Surprised, he held it out to her without thinking. Making a humble gesture of gratefulness, she kissed the hand about to kill her. Murmurs of admiration and pity rose from the crowd. 'Pardon her!' several cried, as though the hapless man had the power to do so. Sanson turned to his son, who had come to Paris for a few days from Pontoise, where he was learning the job under the executioner there, and had accompanied his father in order to see the notorious Madame Tiquet at close quarters.

'Take my place!' croaked the aged executioner to his son. 'My strength is failing me.'

Charles II, as the family called him, grasped the weighty sword his father handed him. For some moments he looked hesitatingly at it. Just then Madame Tiquet said, 'Would you be good enough to tell me how I should put myself?'

'Kneel down with your head up, your hair lifted away from your neck and falling over your face.' Which of the two Sansons replied is not known; but it was a voice that seemed to come from beyond the grave.

Young Charles, too, lost his composure. Only Angélique

remained calm. She arranged her hair as told, knelt down, her body erect, and asked, 'Am I all right like this?'

Just as Charles II, urged on by his father, raised the sword and swung it round his head, the condemned woman cried out (for the first time since reaching the place of execution). 'Be sure not to disfigure me!'

This ultimate feminine thought, this coquettish exclamation, shattered the little courage the young man had mustered. His arms seemed to falter, and the death-dealing weapon fell loosely on the poor woman's ear, cutting it in half and slicing at the cheek. Blood spurted forth, and cries of horror came from the crowd. Angélique toppled forward and plunged about like a wounded horse. One of Sanson's assistants had to hold her legs down on the boards, while old Sanson grasped her by the hair and kept her head still, and then young Charles gave another swipe. But so unnerved was he that the sword only partly cut into the neck. A third stroke was needed to complete the beheading.

And such was the reason for it being written at the time, and later repeated by the few biographers of Madame Tiquet, that the Paris executioner was ill and had called on the Pontoise executioner to replace him, and that the latter showed himself 'little practised at his job.'

On that day, June 19th, 1699, old Sanson turned the last page in his professional life. He wrote out his resignation in the evening, and asked for his son to be appointed his successor.

The authorities made some difficulties, for young Charles had hardly proved his capabilities. Old Sanson pleaded for his son and heir, referring to his own loss of will-power. A public executioner is a man, nevertheless, and to put to death a woman as pretty, as gracious and resigned as Madame Tiquet called for a callousness and a coarseness of mind rarely found in one person. Fortunately for the auxiliary of justice, criminals were usually of a less pleasant aspect.

Sanson's point of view was accepted by the authorities; and although Charles II did not obtain his 'letters of appointment' until after his father's death, he was authorised to replace him until then. Charles I remained the official executioner and was responsible for capital sentences being carried out. It was up to him to instruct his son in the efficient handling of his duties.

Once this favour was obtained, old Sanson turned his mind to marrying again. For some years he had known a master-turner in the rue Beauregard called Pierre Dubut. This craftsman had two daughters, one much older than the other. The elder was a spinster getting on in years, and to put it bluntly was difficult to marry off. But her intelligence and gentle ways, and especially her understanding of Sanson's anguished mind and obsessions, decided the elderly widower in search of tranquillity to offer her his name and wealth. She accepted the task of consoling the man of 64; young Charles saw in Jeanne-Renée Dubut the ideal companion for his father in retirement, and favoured the marriage.

The matter was soon concluded. On Saturday, July 11th, 1699, only 22 days after the execution of Madame Tiquet, Jeanne-Renée Dubut was married to Charles Sanson in her parish church of Notre-Dame-de-Bonne-Nouvelle. She became more a companion than a real wife, and sweetened his last few years.

Old Sanson had become pious almost to the point of mania. He was on very close terms with the vicar of St. Laurent's and attended every service, sunk deep in meditation. He told his family and his few friends that he prayed not for himself but for those he had executed. To him, the justice of men emanated from on high, and God could not punish him for having been the humble instrument for carrying out sentences given in His name. Sanson often repeated Christ's words, 'Blessed are they that mourn.' And he added, 'I've mourned enough to appear before His court confident and trusting when my time comes.'

Every year he gave a dinner at his house on Twelfth Night. He attached great importance to this festivity, which was both a religious and a family occasion. There were usually fifteen people at table, one being some poor person who was specially invited.

Pierre Dubut and his younger daughter were naturally of the number. Her name was Marthe, and she brought the sparkle of youth to the grim looks which betrayed the forbidding profession of the majority of the guests. Charles II was courting her, and she did not seem averse to him.

Gradually, Charles I's obsessions began to return. His wife's presence, which had been so beneficial at the beginning of their married life, no longer sufficed. The sight of a drop of blood gave him a nervous breakdown. He stopped the lessons in anatomy that he was giving his son, and sent away sick people who had heard of his cures and had come to see him.

In spite of having retired, he could not take a step without being reminded of his office. One day he was expressly ordered to be present — still being the holder of the office — at the pillorying of a catch of some quality. It was as a result of this, apparently, that he decided to leave, or rather flee, Paris.

Three magistrates had been sentenced to banishment for selling their influence in the judgment of a certain Marquis des Ferrières. Such a sentence was always preceded by six hours in the pillory. Charles Sanson, obliged to accompany his son, put on his wide-brimmed hat and his red and blue garb with the gibbet and ladder embroidered in black on it, buckled on the sword of justice, and so arrived in front of his old house by the pillory. A great crowd of vagrants, unsavoury gipsies and ragged toughs had already gathered there. The notorious slummy district where they used to live, known as the Cour des Miracles, no longer existed; Louis XIV had caused it to be demolished in 1656. But its forty thousand inhabitants had swarmed together again in several districts farther afield, at Reuilly, the Faubourg du Temple, and on the Butte aux Moulins. And now thousands of them had come from those miserable lairs to see what the three judges would look like standing in the famous revolving pillory to which they had so often sent thieves and vagabonds.

Although the tipstaffs kept the crowd at a distance, they could not prevent the aged executioner from being booed and insulted by the mob. In the past he had hanged, broken on the wheel, or beheaded so many malefactors that their brethren took some revenge by hurling abuse at him.

When he got back home, old Sanson decided to leave Paris. His application to the judicial authorities met with success. He was given permission to move from the capital, and he bought a small farm at Condé-en-Brie, where he went with his wife in 1703.

He died there in May, 1707, at the age of 72. His family had the coffin brought to Paris, and the funeral service was held at St. Laurent's, which was packed to the doors with mourners. There were many public executioners from the provinces and 'questioners' from the Châtelet and other prisons, all jostling with magistrates, people of rank whose rheumatism had been cured by the deceased, burgesses and their wives, and even women of the streets whom old Sanson had helped back to a better life.

He was buried inside the church, next to his first wife; the blank flagstone covering the tomb can still be seen, near a churchwarden's pew.

CHAPTER THREE

Charles II, the perceptive

SUCH A CONCOURSE at the funeral of a public executioner was most unusual. The person and his office, by its very nature, inspired a deep repulsion in his fellow-men. Why should Charles I have been something of an exception? Undoubtedly because he eased the pains of sick people and showed more humane feelings, in his role of executioner, than his predecessors. In addition, it was vaguely known that he had adopted the condition of public executioner through love of someone and to save her honour. These rumours left an impression that the deceased executioner had had two sides to him, one stained with blood, the other coloured in romantic hues. The French have always had a tender spot for lovers.

Rumour had it, too, that men of gentle birth had not been ashamed to dine at Sanson's table; and that lively minds, members of the Academy, had dedicated some of their books to him. Actually, one such dedication seems to have been made — though not to Sanson, but to one of his predecessors, Jean Guillaume. A book by Antoine Furetière was in fact inscribed 'To the most eminent and redoubtable seigneur, Jean Guillaume, master-executioner for Paris.' But as Furetière often made fun of the pompous dedications of his fellow writers by addressing his own 'To No One' or 'To All My Friends,' no doubt his dedication to Guillaume was in similar vein.

In those times, when the death penalty was applied not only to assassins but even to plotters of crime and thieves who had committed no bodily harm, when the pillory and the whip were punishments for minor infractions and for offences against morality and the Church, then the executioner was so much a part of public life, so much in evidence, that the people looked upon him as a necessary evil and could hardly avoid rubbing shoulders with him daily, their repugnance being mixed with respect. Although Charles I had not escaped being treated in this peculiarly inconsistent manner, he had succeeded in asserting himself as a person by his loathing for his functions, his lack of conceit, and his affable manner. His move away from the Pillory house counted for a lot, too, in the slight weakening of public prejudice against him. In addition, his herbal remedies and cures — considered miraculous by some people — earned him the gratitude of his clients.

The whole family was of course at his funeral. Marthe Dubut, his young sister-in-law, had by then also become his daughter-in-law. For some time she had shown affection for the old executioner's son, and the son was well aware that to find a wife outside his confraternity was by no means easy. On April 30th, 1707, just eight days prior to old Sanson's death, Marthe Dubut and Charles II had been married in the church of Notre-Dame-de-Bonne-Nouvelle. The old man was then very ill at Condé-en-Brie and had not been present at the wedding; but had sent his wife to represent him.

Practically all the guests were members of the confraternity or closely connected with it. There was Marguerite Jouenne, the cousin with the same name as the first Madame Sanson; she had been widowed twice, her first husband having been Jean-Baptiste Morin, public executioner at Pontoise, and her second Nicolas Levasseur, whom Charles I had succeeded. There were Nicolas Lemarchand, public executioner at Mantes, and his wife Marie, sister of the deceased Levasseur; Jean Demorets, attached as a 'questioner' to the Paris Parlement; Noel Desmasures, tipstaff at the Châtelet, Pierre Dubut, the bride's father, and his second wife, Elisabeth; Marguerite Guillaume, the widow of the law-officer, André Guillaume, whose brother had been the executioner to whom Furetière had dedicated a book; and Gilles Darboucher, a greengrocer whose wife was the sister of Pierre Dubut's first wife. It was an odd collection; the comment made by the last of the Sansons in his book was: 'It will be seen that although she was twice married, the other Marguerite Jouenne had only been able to find husbands who were public executioners; that Marie Levasseur and Marguerite Guillaume had met with the same lot; and that Marthe Dubut had been unable to make a more brilliant match than her elder sister. The gibbet and the axe had always to be part of the trousseau of these unfortunate young women when they went to the altar.'

Charles II had been granted his father's place by interim in 1703, by letters patent signed on September 8th of that year. After his father's death in 1707 he received his letters of appointment which confirmed him in his functions. The conditions were still the same as in his father's time, including the *droit de havage*.

Thanks to this privilege, Charles II was able to give his wife a princely home. The young couple — he was 26, she 24 — went to live at first with his step-mother, who was also his sister-in-law, in the house hard by St. Anne's church. A few months later Charles and Marthe moved into a mansion that he bought from the heirs of a Monsieur Caignet. It stood at the junction of the rue Bleue and the rue des Poissonniers (today the rue du Faubourg-Poissonnière), and the large garden behind covered an area that now includes the Square Montholon. No doubt mothers of the present day who take their children into this public square and garden would give a little shudder if they realised that for most of a century notorious executioners had strolled over this ground when relaxing at the end of a grisly day. For the property remained in the possession of the Sansons until 1778.

Charles II paid 6,000 *livres* for it in 1708. This was the same amount as his father had paid in 1688 for the *chauffecire* of his letters of appointment. So the extent of the first Sanson's fortune when at Dieppe can be realised. The registration tax — or purchase price — attached to the appointment of public executioner at Paris was the equivalent of a grand, three-floored mansion with a large courtyard in front containing stables, coach-house, and servants' quarters, and grounds with lawns, flower-beds, and trees at the back.

Such were the peaceful surroundings where Charles and his wife lived. Unlike his father, he did not suffer from any obsession; being the son and grandson of public executioners he looked upon his office as fatal and inevitable. And, except for poor Madame Tiquet, he had only executed common rogues and highway robbers who were not worthy of pity.

But after Louis XIV's death in 1715 Charles was called upon to cut short the lives of more important people. This monarch had left France in a precarious situation. His continual wars had ruined the Treasury, and his stupid, wicked revocation of the Edict of Nantes had caused many great merchants and industrialists to flee the country. The Regent, Philippe d'Orléans, was faced with a deficit difficult to meet. To find the money, he summoned the financiers to appear before a court which had the task of finding out how they had made their money. Many bankers subsequently had their fortunes confiscated and were sent to the galleys, but the ten richest were handed over to Sanson for execution.

In the meantime, Charles had become a father. After nine years of childless marriage, Marthe gave birth to a girl in 1716. She was christened Renée-Anne. The poor child was destined from birth to remain within the confraternity. Twenty years later she married the public executioner at Soissons, a man named Zelle, and their male descendants held the post up to the Revolution.

Although the Regent was an atheist and a libertine he believed in the supernatural, provided it was based on occultism. He had an alchemist's study at the Palais Royal, where he resided. One day, an Italian named Planta said he could show him the devil in the quarries at Vanves, and Philippe d'Orléans agreed to go there accompanied only by one of his friends. Unlike his uncle, Louis XIV, the Regent liked going about incognito.

Planta was a spy in the pay of the King of Spain, the uncle of the boy-King of France, Louis XV. With the aid of another tool of the Spanish monarch, a roughneck Baron from Silesia called von Schlieben, Planta had plotted to get the Regent into the

Vanves quarries and for Schlieben to kidnap him, to kill him if he resisted.

By an amazing coincidence, this plot was upset by Charles Sanson.

The German had a mistress in Paris, a woman of about 30 who called herself Antoinette Sicard and said she was the daughter of a middle-class family in the provinces. So lovely was she that she could not go out without men turning to look at her. She rarely left the house where she lodged, in the rue du Pont-aux-Choux, and only then at night and in a carriage. On the other hand, she received so many men visitors that the other tenants thought she must live on her charms. But actually her only visitor was von Schlieben, in a different disguise each time, dressed as an officer or a workman, a priest or a magistrate, to avoid arousing suspicion by his frequent presence. In concert with the thugs he had recruited, Schlieben was waiting the day for his Italian accomplice to decoy the Regent into the quarries.

One evening, Antoinette's neighbours heard loud voices coming from her rooms. The discussion developed into a quarrel; furniture toppled to the floor, blows were struck, and the tone mounted between the supposed harlot and her visitor. Fearing the worst, the neighbours broke in the door. Antoinette, looking mad with rage, was holding a dagger to a purple-faced musketeer. Was she defending herself or threatening the soldier? Without waiting to find out, the neighbours separated the two and disarmed the furious woman.

Law-officers arrived on the scene just after the musketeer — who was none other than von Schlieben — had taken advantage of the uproar to slip away. The young woman was arrested and taken before a lieutenant of police, whose interrogation was all the more cursory as he accepted the statements of the neighbours and took the pretty prisoner for a harlot.

Antoinette could not deny it without revealing the plot against the Regent (which was a capital offence) and so merely maintained she did not know the client who had made off. The officer's powers enabled him to judge a harlot charged with creating a public nuisance, and he sentenced Antoinette Sicard to thirty strokes on the bare back, to stand in the pillory for an hour, and to be imprisoned in the Salpêtrière for an indefinite period.

The pretty young woman was taken to the pillory at the Halles. In the presence of the crowd that soon gathered, eager for the sight, Sanson's assistants stripped her to the waist and attached her wrists to two rings in the wall. When she saw her breasts exposed, Antoinette began to weep. Such unusual modesty surprised Sanson, who was more used to foul language from prostitutes. One of his assistants grasped the whip, and the lashes began to sting the bare back of the helpless prisoner. 'Harder!' 'Lower down!' 'Drop her skirts!' came the shouts from the mob of onlookers. In her pain and shame, Antoinette struggled despairingly and her screams were heart-breaking. As she writhed about, the shimmerings of her naked breasts increased the ribald laughter of the spectators. So much did she wriggle and twist that her hair fell down and a small packet dropped to the ground; it burst open, and a ring and a diamond rolled out. The assistant who was kneeling down holding her ankles to prevent her kicking saw the two gems and swiftly pocketed them.

When he unfastened her to put her in the pillory she murmured between her tears as she drew her clothes on: 'I shan't tell on you; I'll even let you keep the diamond if you'll take the ring to Monsieur Planta, an Italian you'll find at the Duc de Richelieu's town-house. He will give you what it's worth; tell him not to forget me when the time comes.'

The varlet promised, and took his prisoner up to the pillory. For the next hour, her lovely head clamped tight, Antoinette endured this second humiliation. Her back and loins were smarting from the whipping. At last she was freed, and a constable took her off to the Salpêtrière prison.

It was then that Charles Sanson noticed the ring on his assistant's finger. 'What's that?' he demanded, grasping the man's hand and examining the piece of jewellery; there was a coat of arms on the ring, and it seemed very valuable.

The assistant went red, admitted picking it up and repeated what the young woman had said to him. Sanson snatched the ring and the diamond from him, and thought for a moment. The arms on the ring intrigued him. Did the name Antoinette Sicard conceal the identity of a great lady? If so, he thought, there's a conspiracy behind all this. Taking his assistant with him, Sanson hurried off to see the lieutenant and tell his story.

The young woman was fetched 'from the Salpêtrière and confronted with the thief. When she was threatened with being put to the question if she did not explain her mysterious message, she revealed that Planta was something of a magician, that the musketeer was von Schlieben, and the two were planning to kidnap or assassinate 'a leading personality' in the quarries at Vanves, enticing him there by promising an apparition of the Devil.

The officer was unaware that the Regent was the person concerned, but nevertheless informed the *abbé* Dubois, who was a Counsellor of State and had been the Regent's tutor. This priest knew his ex-pupil only too well, and at once guessed the rest. Orders went out for the arrest of the Italian and the German; Planta succeeded in fleeing the country, but von Schlieben was captured while crossing the Pyrenees. He was brought back to Paris and thrown into the Bastille. And his mistress was released from the Salpêtrière prison. She had no doubt revealed her real name — one of the most aristocratic in France, according to the few in the know.

As for Charles Sanson, he was allowed to keep the ring as a reward for being so perceptive. And his descendants, for more than a hundred years, produced it on occasion as proof of their loyalty to the Crown.

That was not the only time Charles Sanson showed himself to be perceptive . . .

Philippe d'Orléans devoted himself to his duties as Regent during the daytime, but then his unhealthy tastes for debauchery took control. At five in the evening, the gates of the Palais Royal were firmly locked and the Court's 'relaxation' began. Through the servants, the public had a good idea of what this 'relaxation' meant. The words 'orgy', 'bacchanalian feast', and 'incest', went

from mouth to mouth; and, distorted and enlarged on by scand-
alised rumour, gave the Regent the reputation of being some
salacious potentate. There was exaggeration in all this, no doubt;
but descriptions of the 'supper parties by bell' at the Palais Royal
reached the ears of Sanson, as of so many other people. He was
to remember them in circumstances far from ordinary.

The Regent and his guests ate unattended and the servants
only entered at the ring of a hand-bell — because the women
guests were in the costume of Eve. They were not women of the
town but ladies of rank, who — according to popular belief —
found it entertaining to sit naked at table between gentlemen
fully dressed. The names mentioned were the Comtesse de
Parabère, the Regent's recognised mistress, and her rival, the
Marquise de Sabran; Mesdames de Falari, de Gesvres, du Deffand,
and others of equally good family, and even the Duchess of
Berry, the Regent's own daughter.

The Comtesse de Parabère excelled in organising these erotic
feasts. With peculiar modesty, she had taffeta capes placed over
the backs of the ladies' chairs, her own included. When Philippe
d'Orléans rang the bell to summon the servants, the women
guests used the capes to draw a veil over their consciences. These
proud creatures found it pleasing to reveal their charms to
men of their own class, but were ashamed to show as much to
lackeys.

These delightful parties were the subject of many a laugh and
jest among the crowds outside John Law's Bank in the rue
Quincampoix, where great ladies rubbed shoulders with seam-
stresses, and princes with porters. Women wearing taffeta capes
found themselves being asked by bold wags: 'Do you by any
chance have dinner by bell?'

The Regent hoped to replenish the Treasury and bring prosper-
ity to the country through Law's financial system. But, fanned
by virulent pamphlets, the scandals of Philippe's private life and
the attacks on his financial innovations lost him the popularity
he had had at the end of Louis XIV's reign. Law's financial
enemies were trying to ruin the bank by creating a sort of bear
market. They presented several million banknotes for payment,

and dividends dropped from forty to two per cent. The shareholders started to sell out, and the Regent's enemies began to
exult.

Yet Philippe d'Orléans was not without certain qualities;
he governed France wisely, renouncing the warlike policy of
Louis XIV and encouraging economic expansion. Voltaire said of
him: 'The only reproach that could be made against this Prince
was his taste for pleasure and novelty. Of all Henri IV's descendants, Philippe d'Orléans was the one most like him; he had the
same good nature and indulgence, the gaiety, ease, and candour,
with a more cultivated mind.' Like Henri IV too, he believed in
tolerance and considered a Protestant, a Jew, or an atheist, to be
as much a man as a Catholic. This spirit of tolerance was to be
the cause of Sanson calling to mind the stories of the 'suppers by
bell' and having the one terrible, alarming experience that could
compare, all due allowance made, to the anguish suffered by his
father.

John Law's bank, then, collapsed early in 1720. Panic-stricken
shareholders rushed there to claim their money. The Duc de
Bourbon and the Prince de Conti came out with millions in gold
that they stowed into their carriages. The Duc d'Antin exchanged
his shares for rolls of cloth, the Duc d'Estrées his for some tons
of chocolate, while the Duc de la Force got all the candles in
Paris with his. People fought to sell their shares, just as they had
fought to buy them. A young nobleman belonging to a great
family, the Comte Antoine de Horn, who was a grandson of the
Prince de Ligne and a cousin of the Regent, enticed a market-
jobber into a tavern in the rue de Venise by proposing to sell him
shares worth 100,000 crowns; and then stabbed him and stole
his wallet. But the noise of his struggles with Antoine de Horn
and the latter's accomplice, the Chevalier de Mille, brought a
server hurrying to the room. Seeing one of the three streaming
with blood, he shut the door and called for help.

The two assassins jumped out of the window, but were soon
caught, arrested, and thrown into prison. As murder had obviously
been committed, they were brought before the court a few days
later. The Chevalier de Mille admitted everything, even that the

crime had been premeditated. But the Comte de Horn pleaded an excuse in the fact that the victim was a Jew.

The magistrates referred the case to the *abbé* Dubois, who consulted the Regent. Philippe retorted, 'Let the law take its course.'

It was pointed out to him that Antoine de Horn and the Chevalier could only be sentenced to the most ignoble of deaths, to be broken on the wheel. The shame of it would touch the whole family, including the Regent himself. To which he quoted a verse of Thomas Corneille: 'The crime makes the shame, not the scaffold.'

The Regent had given proof of his attitude of equal justice towards Jews some eighteen months previously. An Alsatian Jew named Nordemann had been imprisoned in Basle, where he often went on business. No reason had been given, unless it were his origin and religion. When the Regent heard of this arbitrary arrest he sent the Duc d'Avaray with the mission of obtaining Nordemann's release. The archives of the State of Basle still contain d'Avaray's written protest, requesting the Jew's release 'in the name of the Roy de France'.

In his attitude towards the Protestants, too, Philippe showed himself liberal-minded and in advance of his time. He dared not re-establish the Edict of Nantes, but he did give instructions to his administrators in the southern provinces that the Protestants were to be allowed to meet as they wished. In Paris, where the Jews practised their religion within the intimacy of the family circle, the Regent showed his intention of authorising them to build a synagogue.

Philippe d'Orléans could not pardon his cousin, the murderer of a Jew, and remain consistent to this attitude. The judges therefore condemned Antoine de Horn to be broken on the wheel, but thought the Regent would reprieve him.

All Paris took a great interest in the case, and Charles Sanson especially, as he was involved in its conclusion. On the evening of March 23rd (1720) he was strolling round his garden when a servant came running up to him.

'Master,' he cried, 'there's a lady asking to see you, and she refuses to give her name!'

Sanson had her shown into the salon, and then told his servant to leave them. A black veil covered the visitor's face, and a black cloak hid her dress. Charles asked the reason for her visit. In a tragic tone she replied: 'Would you believe it? I've been unable to obtain his reprieve. A youngster of twenty-two! They've vowed he shall die! They want to hand him over to you. To you!'

Sanson gave a gesture of incomprehension, but she went on more wildly. 'It's driving me mad! I fled from that cursed Palais Royal because I was so furious. I loathe all three of them — that toady of an *abbé*, that great fool of a Scot, and a prince even more cynical! Ah, do they think they're going to regild their useless money in this child's blood! He's only twenty-two. They're despicable.!'

The word 'child' caused Sanson to think he was listening to Antoine de Horn's mother — the executioner guessed he was the person she was talking about. But when Sanson risked an allusion to such a relationship he was rewarded by a savage laugh. At the same time the stranger snatched off her veil and let her cloak fall to the floor. A ravishing young woman in court dress stood revealed to the executioner, who was even more amazed when she announced: 'Look at me — I am the Comtesse de Parabère, the Regent's mistress!'

Charles stifled an exclamation. The low dress, beribboned and adorned with jewels, showed off her lovely shoulders. She had a slender neck and an oval, full face, the large eyes now blazing with fury and proud awareness of her irresistible beauty.

All the rumours and popular stories connected with her came surging into the public executioner's mind. He could not help undressing her with his eyes and imagining her sitting naked at a 'supper by bell.'

'You see,' she said, having weighed her powers of seduction, and addressing Sanson in the intimate *tu*. 'You see I put on my most beautiful clothes in order to please him, in order to charm this prince who dares to share his favours between me and the Sabran. But it was of no use. When I spoke to him about this poor lad and the illustrious families he's related to, the Regent merely sent for Dubois and Law. Ah, executioner, if you had seen what happened then! If you had heard what they said! They don't care about the poor Jew who was killed. What matters to them is tolerance, paper-money, the system, public credit, and I don't know what. That's how they replied to my appeals. I couldn't stand it, I left the Palais Royal banging the door behind me. I've come straight here, for you're the only hope I have left. You'll save my Antoine de Horn, won't you? Say you'll save him . . .'

This flow of words disclosed much to Charles Sanson. The Comtesse de Parabère, then, who reproached the Regent for 'sharing his favours', returned the compliment by sleeping with the Comte de Horn. The most inglorious of Frenchmen, the public executioner, was stepping straight into the intimate life of the highest in the land.

He thought a moment. 'Madam,' he replied, 'I'm as powerless to save anyone as to bring about their undoing. I'm not a man, but a sword. Monseigneur the Regent has the right of reprieve, I only have the right of execution.'

'You can let him escape!' she retorted.

'My duty prevents me doing that.'

'Your duty . . .! Listen — my friends will arrange for your cart to be attacked on its way from the Conciergerie to the Place de Grève. Don't make any resistance, nor stop him getting away, and you'll be rewarded.'

'What should I do with the money? My house shows how large my income is. The monarchs have always ensured that the public executioners were well off, so that they should be above corruption. In my sad position, I must remain deaf and dumb, blind, unmoved. Haven't I taken the oath?'

'Nonsense! Ask anything you like from me. Riches never refuse to be added to! Would you like some gold? Here, take this packet — there are a hundred *louis* in it. The day after the escape, come and see me — and I'll give you ten times as much!'

Charles pushed away the hand holding out the packet.

'What do you want, then?' exclaimed the Countess. 'I repeat, come and see me the day after the escape — no, the same evening. You know I'm a kind of Queen, in a way — well then, I give you my word as a Queen, you can have anything you want! I'll give you all, d'you hear, all!'

Sanson, though more amazed than ever, did not lose grip. Pretending not to have understood what the Countess was offering him, he gave a pitying smile as he replied, 'Keep your gold, Madam. It's not my function to guard against an attempt to rescue condemned prisoners. They are watched by the troops escorting my cart. However, I can promise you . . .' He hesitated, and seemed to be considering something.

'What?' asked the Countess, hopeful again.

'Not to prevent Monsieur de Horn from escaping if your friends succeed in their attack on the cart.'

In spite of himself, the incorruptible had been influenced by his visitor's charms. Charles Sanson felt an enormous pleasure; he, the bloodstained functionary from whom people turned in disgust, had been offered an hour of love by the Regent's mistress. Such awful humiliation for her, such a bright revenge for him, was well worth a promise that cost nothing and that he would not be called upon to keep, because of the number of troops protecting the cart.

She thanked him warmly for this valueless agreement. Then, suddenly realising perhaps how vain were her hopes, she said in a gasping voice: 'If my friends are unable to bribe the jailers . . . if they fail through some cowardice at the last minute . . . if they don't overcome the guards of that infamous Dubois . . . then promise me you'll murmur my name in the Count's ear before he goes to meet his God, and that you'll send me something of his to remember him by, which I'll keep all my life.'

'I promise you that, Madam.'

She burst into tears, stammered her thanks, and made to gather up her cloak which had been lying at her feet all this time. Charles, like a gallant gentleman, was the quicker; he helped her to put it on, and then escorted her out to her coach.

While the Comtesse de Parabère was making this humiliating and difficult attempt, 57 members of the condemned man's family were presenting a 'Petition from the relatives of the Prince de

Horn and of the Comte de Horn to Monseigneur the Regent'. Among the signatures were those of the Prince de Ligne, the Duc de Montmorency, Monsieur d'Harcourt and Monsieur de Créquy, the Prince de Soubise, the Duc de la Force, the Burgrave of Leyde, the Princess de Croy, and the Dowager Duchess de Goyon.

The signatories affirmed that Antoine de Horn was mentally unbalanced. They recalled that his paternal uncle, Ambroise de Horn, was insane and had been confined in his own château for the past seventeen years; that his maternal uncle, Ferdinand de Ligne, was also mad and had been confined for the past three years; and that his grandfather on his mother's side had died after losing his reason. The petition went on to say that the condemned man had himself 'been attacked by an illness that physicians in Brabant and also the judiciary authorities of the Austrian Low Countries recognised as possessing all the characteristics of mental derangement.' And the petition ended by asking the Regent to reprieve the guilty man.

For the first time in history, a criminal's heredity was presented as an excuse for his crime. The 57 signatories went in a body to the Palais Royal, but the Regent would only receive a deputation. He read the petition in their presence, but his attitude remained frigid.

Having been unable to make the Master waver, the Count's relatives thought of the most ignoble of his servants. Monsieur de Créquy went and called at the public executioner's house. He was received by Charles in the salon where the Comtesse de Parabère had humbled herself to the point of offering her body. The visitor asked the executioner to repeat his promise not to resist an attack. Sanson did so, but refused the hundred *louis* that the other, like the Countess, tried to make him accept.

That evening Sanson received orders to execute Antoine de Horn and the Chevalier de Mille the following morning. He read the instructions closely, believing the last lines would contain the secret order to apply the *retentum*. This measure was rarely granted; it saved the condemned person from suffering agonies on the wheel. He was strangled surreptitiously with a cord, so that the iron clubs were only breaking the bones of a corpse.

All that night Marthe prayed for the souls of her husband's next two victims. At dawn, Sanson set off with his cart and material and his assistants for the Conciergerie, from where he would take the Count and the Chevalier to the nearby Place de Grève. He found them in a pitiful state; they had undergone the torture that preceded every execution, to obtain names of accomplices. The iron boot had been applied to the eighth turn of the screw, and had crushed their ankles; neither of them could stand.

Sanson's assistants carried them out to his cart. As they were being laid on the straw, Charles whispered in the young Count's ear: 'Don't give up hope. You know much is being done to save you. Your relatives are busy, the Comtesse de Parabère is moving heaven and earth. If an attack is made, I shan't do anything.'

The cart moved off towards the Hôtel de Ville surrounded by a strong armed guard. People stood massed along the houses on the Pont-au-Change and the quays. Sanson looked at the crowd without apprehension. He knew the expected attack would not take place; his perceptiveness made him sure of that. There were, he thought, more fainthearts than men of action among the Count's relatives. When the cart reached the Place de Grève, Antoine de Horn said in a weak voice, 'Tell the Comtesse I forgive her. Only her.'

The two young men were each tied to a St. Andrew's cross placed flat on a wheel, and then Sanson hurled an order to his assistants. Two of them seized massive iron clubs and started to smash the limbs of the criminals. The Chevalier de Mille cried out horribly, but the other remained silent; Sanson had illegally applied the *retentum*, and his chief assistant, Nicolas Gros, was only smashing at a dead man.

Aware of the different treatment meted out to the two criminals, Charles decided to cut short the Chevalier's sufferings. He glanced up at the balcony of the Parloir aux Bourgeois, at the magistrate delegated to be present at the execution. This official, no doubt having little taste for such a spectacle, was standing with his back turned to Sanson and chatting with some women. In the crowded square other women were giving cries of horror as the blows thudded down. Their exclamations mingled with de Mille's bellows of agony.

'That's enough,' Sanson cried to Gros. 'Go and put an end to the other one!'

Nicolas Gros left off hitting at the corpse and went over to de Mille; pushing the other assistant aside, he dropped a heavy block of iron on the Chevalier's chest, smashing it and bursting the heart open. And so two corpses were left stretched on the horizontal wheels; usually, the mangled men lingered on for an hour or two before expiring.

In the afternoon, the Comtesse de Parabère received an envelope sent by Sanson. The words 'Promised souvenir' were written on it, and inside she found a lock of the Comte de Horn's hair.

Charles Sanson saw this celebrated mistress of the Regent again, in different circumstances. One October evening in 1721 he went to the Châtelet prison to have a look at Cartouche, the notorious highwayman who was shortly to be tried. A long queue was waiting to get into the prison; everyone wanted to be able to say 'I've seen him!' And the authorities, with the object of reassuring the public and dissuading others from imitating Cartouche's exploits, had issued masses of permits to visit the prison. Among the people edging through the gates of the Châtelet Sanson noticed a working-girl accompanied by two modestly-dressed men. He recognised the three, in spite of their disguise; they were the Comtesse de Parabère and two gentlemen, Messieurs de Tresnel and de Nocé.

Near the end of November, Sanson took Cartouche to the Place de Grève. As he set off in his cart he called to the crowd to let him through, using the traditional phrase — 'Make way for the King's justice!'

In the course of his life, Charles Sanson was often called upon to execute 'the King's justice.' It would be pointless, and sickening, to give the long list of victims. The scaffold and the gibbet were not left idle during the minority of Louis XV. The rest of Cartouche's band perished on the wheel after him, but the two women named Néron and Jeanneton who had been the favourites of his harem dangled at the end of a rope. On that busy day the people who lived in the tragic Place de Grève did good business, letting their windows to the highest bidders.

Marthe had in the meantime given birth to two more children. Charles-Jean-Baptiste was born in April, 1719, and Nicolas-Charles-Gabriel in May, 1721. With Renée-Anne, born in 1716, there were thus five in the Sanson family.

For several years the father had been having difficulties with his superiors over the *droit de havage*. So many complaints arose over the collecting of this levy that the Paris Parlement was considering its suppression. Charles II increased his efforts and applications for the ancient privilege to be maintained. But in the end he was unsuccessful. On October 1st, 1721, the Regent signed a decree abolishing the *droit de havage* in Paris, replacing it with a salary of 16,000 *livres* a year, to come from Treasury funds.

Charles at once requested an audience of the Regent, who received him at the Palais Royal and listened to his grievances. The executioner's case was soon stated. The discredit attached to his position prevented his sons from leaving the confraternity and his daughters from marrying outside it; the fifty or sixty thousand *livres* that the *droit de havage* produced were a modest compensation for being rejected by society.

The Regent admitted the force of the argument. Yet he could not go back on his signature, disdain the considered opinion of his Parlement, and increase the salary already fixed.

'Let the matter rest for a while,' he said to Sanson, 'and in the meantime I will make you a present.' And the Regent gave orders for the petitioner to be handed 50,000 *livres* in notes issued by Law's bank.

'But these notes aren't worth anything now,' the executioner protested.

'Bah!' replied the Regent. 'They'll recover their value one day.'

It was doubtful; so much, in fact, that Charles's descendants still had the notes a century and a half later.

On Charles's insistence, the Regent consented to the executioner having more of condemned persons' clothing. Until then, public executioners had been allowed to keep everything worn above the waist; from now on, they could take all they found on the body and sell the effects as they wished.

Charles also obtained a fixed fee of five *sous* for every execution, like his colleagues in the provinces. Finally, he was allowed an indemnity each time he had to operate away from the pillory by the Halles or the Place de Grève — whenever he placed a person in the pillory called *L'Echelle* in the rue St. Honoré (on the corner of the present rue de l'Echelle), or whipped a woman outside the entrance to the Salpêtrière prison, or a man in the square in front of the Palais de Justice; and on the rare occasions when he had to perform one of his functions in the outskirts of Paris.

All these additional attributes only supplemented his salary by five or six thousand *livres* a year. As he wanted to live on the same scale as before, he added to his income by practising the quack medicine he had learnt from his father. He was able to give himself over to this; popular belief was that no healer was as good as the public executioner. He left it to his assistants to put malefactors in the pillory, to administer whippings and apply brandings, and only appeared himself at executions.

He worked so much at his remedies for the sick and ailing that his health began to decline. When the Regent died in December, 1723, Charles said to his wife, 'It will soon be my turn.' Marthe gently chided him.

But three years later, when only 45, he had to take to his bed. Marthe gave him every care; he was still ill, however, when orders came for him to supervise a form of execution that had become rare — burning at the stake.

A minor nobleman from Lorraine named Benjamin des Chauffours had been tried and sentenced to death for homosexual practices. This perversion was then considered a major crime, on a par with heresy — although the Regent's father, brother of Louis XIV, had been a notorious pervert. If Benjamin des Chauffours had only been concerned with one or two others, the law might well have turned a blind eye. But the police had found a list of about 200 men's names in his lodgings, some of them of the higher nobility, for whom he acted as procurer. All these people could not be consigned to the flames, so Chauffours alone was arrested to that end. The warrant for his execution contained mention of the *retentum*, which only the public executioner had the right to apply.

On May 24th, 1726, Sanson got up from his sick-bed to carry out this execution. It was his last appearance in public. Some unknown disease had him in its grip, and he went back to his bed never to rise from it again.

In September he heard the Reaper knocking at his door. His elder son, Charles-Jean-Baptiste, was not yet eight years old. He wanted to make sure of the boy's future, and on September 9th asked Marthe to send for Maître Dupuis, a lawyer at the Châtelet, and two 'questioners', François Prud'homme and Jules Tronson, who were friends of Charles.

The three men came to his bedside. At his request, the lawyer drew up a document by which Charles II transferred his office to his elder son; Jules Tronson was to be his guide and mentor, and François Prud'homme to act for him until the boy was old enough to take over.

Three days later, on September 12th, 1726, Charles Sanson the Second passed away at the age of 45.

He was buried in the church of St. Laurent. All the clergy of the parish were at the funeral, and the mourners were almost as numerous as at his father's burial nineteen years previously. His coffin was placed next to those of his parents. The Sansons thus had, like great lords, their family tomb in a splendid Paris church. Can this unusual honour be regarded as a proof of their nobility and their rights to the seigniory of Longval? Their descendants always claimed so, but no confirmation has ever been produced.

CHAPTER FOUR

Jean-Baptiste, the paralytic

RENEE, Charles I's widow, urged her sister Marthe, Charles II's widow, to take advantage of the extreme youth of her two sons and refuse their father's office. His premature death gave the two boys, aged five and seven, an unexpected chance to escape the family fate.

Marthe was not of the same mind. As the daughter of a respectable master-craftsman she had not feared to marry her sister's son-in-law, nineteen years before, and so in her turn join the coterie of public executioners and their families. Nothing had forced her to do so, unless it were the love she felt for Charles. But now she was a widow she resolved that her youngsters would follow in their father's footsteps. She thought they would be ashamed of him if they did not become executioners in turn.

Fearing that the Parlement might not accept the document signed by her husband on his death-bed, Marthe went to see the procurator-general and the *lieutenant-criminel*. The two magistrates, faced with this rather ruthless mother draped in her widow's weeds and defending the gory future of her sons with a classical stoicism, soon agreed to help her. The matter was decided in her favour, and Jean-Baptiste was appointed public executioner.

At seven years of age!

Of course, François Prud'homme would act for him until he was old enough, 'in a fit state', to perform the functions himself. Nevertheless, the boy would have to be present at capital executions, to legalize them.

In fact, Jean-Baptiste only rarely appeared on the scaffold where Prud'homme was executing in his name; for some years he was represented by his guardian-mentor, Jules Tronson. To enable him to get used to his future functions he was first taken to see people put in the pillory, then to be present at whippings and brandings. Later, he watched executions by hanging, in the Place de Grève, then beheadings and finally the terrible agonies of men being broken on the wheel. By the time he was eighteen, Jean-Baptiste was capable of supervising in person, and took the oath of office.

In the meantime, his mother had married again. Her second husband was Jean-Baptiste Barré, one of the 'questioners' employed by the Paris Parlement. It could be said that she was marrying beneath her. These 'questioners' who tortured prisoners to get them to confess, were the lowest in the abominable hierarchy of which the public executioners were the head. A place as 'questioner' cost less than the office of executioner. The former applied the iron boot, the water torture and the strappado to make the guilty — and even the innocent — talk, while the latter inflicted death on them. The public executioner, moreover, possessed the right of life or death over his own children. The Sansons never availed themselves of this incredible prerogative, which although nowhere confirmed in writing was sanctioned by tradition. But the first of them had almost witnessed it applied — when Pierre Jouenne, at the *Clos Mauduit*, had threatened to kill his daughter if the lieutenant refused to marry her, the Dieppe executioner was within his rights.

Jean-Baptiste Sanson regarded his mother's marriage to a torturer as only partly a degrading match. For Barré was officially allowed the title of *bourgeois de Paris* — a citizen who could take part in the administration of the city; and that made up for the other. Peculiar customs, and peculiar times!

Marthe brought up her three children in the large house in the rue des Poissonniers, always keeping in mind the future she had planned for them. Renée-Anne would marry a public executioner; Jean-Baptiste would be the one in Paris, and Gabriel one somewhere in the provinces, provided a vacancy occurred and could be bought for him. He did, in fact, become public executioner at Rheims.

Jean-Baptiste began to carry out executions himself in 1737, when he was eighteen. Contrary to his mother's expectations, he showed little inclination for the task. After each execution he got out his horse and galloped for hours through the countryside, trying in this way to forget the grisly minutes he had spent on the scaffold. He often called at the home of his old mentor, Jules Tronson, whose daughter Madeleine always tried to comfort him. The two had known each other from childhood. She was only a few months the younger, and being the daughter of a 'questioner' understood all the better the tragedy of the boy destined to become an executioner. When Jean-Baptiste was nineteen he asked for Madeleine's hand in marriage; Jules Tronson gave his consent, and the wedding took place in the church of St. Laurent.

On the evening of the wedding, a dinner with dancing to follow was given at the Sanson house. All the family and friends were there; the executioner's assistants had put on their servants' livery, and a string-quartet was playing. If it had not been for the hard, melancholy expressions in the eyes of some of the male guests, a visitor might have believed himself at the wedding-party of a wealthy bourgeois playing the gentleman.

Outside it was raining in torrents — predicting a happy marriage, according to a French saying.

A servant went up to Jean-Baptiste. 'Master, there are three young noblemen in the ante-room. They lost their way, not knowing this district, and ask to be allowed to shelter here until the rain stops.'

Jean-Baptiste left his wife and guests and went to see the waiting men. One of them wore the uniform of an army lieutenant. 'Monsieur,' he said to Jean-Baptiste, 'pray excuse our temerity. We lost our way in the dark, and were splashing along when we saw your lighted windows and heard the music. As we had no fear of arousing a sleeping household, we came to beg your hospitality. May I know the reason for this party?'

'It's my wedding, gentlemen.'

'Our congratulations!'

'Invite us to join you, then,' the officer added gaily. 'If only to provide your young ladies with three more dancers!'

'It would be a pleasure, something to be very proud of — three noblemen at my wedding! Unfortunately, I fear that my family and guests are not worthy of such an honour.'

'Bah! This is the age of reason and good sense. Come along!'

And without even asking Jean-Baptiste his name, the three cast off their cloaks, brushed their boots with their gloves, and entered the salon. They were a little drunk, the wedding guests too, so introductions were rather swamped. They hardly noticed the sinister aspect of a few of the men; several women were pretty, which was ample compensation. The three danced until midnight, and only thought of leaving on seeing the other guests saying their farewells.

'Well now,' said the lieutenant, 'at least we ought to know whom to thank?'

This was the moment their host had been waiting for, happy to get his revenge for the three's impudence.

'The executioner of criminal sentences, monsieur,' he replied with a sardonic smile. 'I am Jean-Baptiste Sanson, public executioner for the Paris region.'

The three young men went white. 'What a joke!' said one.

'I'm not joking! And I'll tell you this as well, for your edification — most of my guests have the same function in the provinces. Others put the question, or are tipstaffs. Only a few are in trade.'

For some moments he enjoyed their discomfiture. But then the officer gave a laugh. 'What a lucky chance! We might be able to see your collection of instruments of torture! Would you be gallant enough to show us?'

The intruder found pleasure, like a true nobleman, in delaying a commoner's wedding-night. Jean-Baptiste made no objection. Although upset at keeping his young bride waiting, he led the three brazen young men to the shed where he stored his material. He showed them the wheels, the ropes, the iron clubs and the axes and the chopping-blocks, and especially the heavy, double-edged sword with the word *Justicia* engraved on the blade.

The officer tried the edge with his finger. 'With a weapon like this,' he said, 'you're sure of taking off a head in one stroke!'

'Yes indeed!' Jean-Baptiste replied banteringly. 'And if ever

the same fate as the Marquis de Cinq-Mars hung over your
lordship I give you my word here and now that, as I can't let one
of my assistants behead a nobleman, I'd not need two attempts
nor let you languish!'

This joking remark had a bad effect on the young officer. His
smile vanished and a shadow passed over his face, like the sign
of some presentiment. 'Come along!' he cried to his friends,
making for the door.

Sanson escorted them to the street. 'May I have the pleasure,'
he asked, 'of knowing the names of the gentlemen who honoured
my wedding-party with their presence?'

The officer was the only one who deigned to reply. 'I am
Comte Albert-Thomas de Lally-Tollendal,' he said.

As the years went by, Jean-Baptiste gradually forgot his early
aversion to his office of executioner. He became resigned to his
fate, and grew as stern and forbidding as his mother. He believed,
or pretended to believe, it was the will of Providence that the
Sansons should all wield the sword of justice; and he imparted
this belief to his children.

His wife Madeleine produced a child nearly every year, and
eventually there were ten in all, seven boys and three girls. The
three eldest boys, Charles-Henri, Louis-Cyr-Charlemagne, and
Charles-Martin, were destined to earn a woeful notoriety during
the French Revolution . . .

Their father led an orderly life. He rose early, and went to Low
Mass at St. Laurent's. When no execution obliged him to go out,
he spent the morning treating sick people or working in his
dispensary, preparing ointments and plasters for his clients. The
reputation as healers left by his father and grandfather enhanced
his own.

One day, the Comte de Charolais, a son of the Prince de
Condé, arrived at his door in a splendid coach. Two lackeys drew
from it a stretcher bearing a young man groaning with pain. He
was the Count's armourer and sword-cutler, by the name of
Chesneau, and had accidentally wounded himself while handling

an ornamental carbine. It had exploded, breaking his wrist, smashing his chest, and perforating his cheeks.

Jean-Baptiste extracted the bits of metal and dressed the wounds. He kept Chesneau at his house for two months, treating him until he eventually recovered. During this time, Comte de Charolais often came to see his armourer, and chatted with Sanson. He found the executioner different from the popular idea of him; and, appreciating his capabilities as a bone-setter, gave him good publicity at Court. As a result, Jean-Baptiste found his clientele increased by several titled persons.

Then he himself fell gravely ill. In 1754, when he was 34, he was attacked by paralysis. Madeleine called in some of the best physicians in Paris, but they could do nothing for him. Deprived of his movements, though he could still talk, Jean-Baptiste had to resign his office.

His eldest son, Charles-Henri, was not quite fifteen. Although tall and strong for his age, there could be no question of him replacing his father without the aid of the valuable assistants. As soon as news of Jean-Baptiste's incapacity had reached the confraternity in the provinces, several public executioners hurried to Paris to solicit his office.

Madeleine looked upon these competitors with a favourable eye. 'If only,' she thought, 'Charles-Henri could escape this terrible inheritance.' But her mother-in-law, redoubtable old Marthe, would have been ashamed for the grandson not to wield the axe. Silencing her daughter-in-law's objections, she took the lad by the hand and, repeating her efforts years previously on behalf of her son, went to see the procurator-general.

As she entered the magistrate's room, he was dismissing two competitors. Red with anger, he cried to a police-officer, 'Take these men back to their inn! If they haven't left Paris in two hours, lock them up in the Châtelet prison!'

Marthe recognised the applicants — two Jouennes, father and son, distant cousins of the Sansons. They had offered the procurator-general a bribe of 24,000 *livres*, in the hope of getting the vacant place — so much was it worth still, in spite of the *havage* levy having been suppressed.

Marthe was once again successful in her endeavours. Charles-Henri was authorised by the Parlement to replace his father, though he was not invested legally with the office. There was always the possibility that Jean-Baptiste might recover; meanwhile, so long as his paralysed father was alive, Charles-Henri was to act officially as deputy public executioner — a novice of fifteen.

His first execution was in January, 1755, when a certain Ruxton was broken on the wheel. Young Charles-Henri was duly present, turning his head away while his assistants performed their horrible task. Three days later it was the turn of a man named Mongeot, for murdering the husband of his mistress, Madame Lescombat. This execution was not held in the Place de Grève, but at the Croix Rouge crossroads, thus called because in fact a red stone cross stood there. It was snowing heavily; Charles-Henri was shivering with fright and cold, keeping as far along the scaffold as possible from the mulatto smashing at the condemned man. There were few spectators, because of the cold; but Charles-Henri's grandmother was present, standing in the slush and encouraging him to watch the proceedings.

When Mongeot's mangled body was left to expire, being slowly covered with snow, the widow Lescombat was led on to the scaffold. She had been found guilty of inciting Mongeot to kill her husband, and was to be hanged; but as she claimed she was pregnant, the sentence had been suspended for two months. Now she was being pushed forward to look upon the snow-covered, bloody mess that had been her lover, in the hope that the sight would cause her heart to repent and her lips to tell the truth.

As soon as he set eyes on her, Charles-Henri flinched and recoiled. He was at an age when sexual instinct is quickly aroused; and Madame Lescombat, who had kept a restaurant in the rue Garancière, near the Luxembourg palace, was celebrated for her beauty. In spite of her paleness, the youngster was thrown into confusion by the woman's loveliness — no, it couldn't be, it wasn't possible that this marvellous creature was to be hanged! Charles-Henri revolted at the thought, a shudder went through him. As he stared at the woman, who was being forced by a constable to look upon the body, he heard her pretty mouth utter an unexpected remark: 'Well I never! They've put his head at his feet!'

Because of the snow covering the moribund, she was mistaking his legs for his arms. Her comment revealed her for what she was; in the presence of the unfortunate man who had committed murder for her, that was all she could find to say.

She was taken away to the cart, back to prison. Then another woman's voice was heard, that of Marthe calling to her grandson. 'You heard what she said?' As though to convince him that the guilty woman was not worth any compassion.

Charles-Henri saw Madame Lescombat again, two months later. In the Place de Grève this time, and before a great crowd of spectators. Having been lectured by his grandmother and hardened by other executions in the meantime, Charles-Henri watched without flinching the guilty, lovely creature being strung up. He was at last immune against sentiment.

His sixteenth birthday was still a few weeks away.

This proof of her grandson's courage was a great triumph for old Marthe. At 72 years of age she was a real matriarch. Her daughter-in-law was obliged to bend to her iron will; poor Madeleine had lost hope of her children escaping the grim heritage. They, the sons, grandsons, and great-grandsons of executioners, would themselves become executioners. Marthe insisted on it; and Jean-Baptiste, confined to his wheel-chair, was dominated by his terrible mother.

Marthe lived for many more years, and saw all her grandchildren set up. Her pride at the eldest obtaining the office of Paris executioner was increased when the second became executioner at Provins. The other five became executioners at Tours, Blois, Rennes, Orléans, and Montpellier. One of the granddaughters married a cousin who was executioner at Rheims, and the other two found husbands in the executioners at Etampes and at Meaux.

Being thus scattered all over France, the members of this

singular family could not easily meet together. But even when
Marthe was in her eighties she made sure they kept in touch,
insisting on them all dining together at least twice a year at the
big house in the Faubourg Poissonnière. When they were all
gathered round the large table, the servants found it difficult to
remember their proper names, and addressed the men by the town
where each officiated — *Monsieur de Paris, Monsieur de Blois,
Monsieur de Rheims,* and so on. This custom eventually spread
beyond the family circle; so much so, that when there was but a
sole public executioner for the whole of France — the one based
on Paris — the public called him *Monsieur de Paris* as a matter
of course.

These dinners to which 25 or 30 people sat down were presided
over by old Marthe, with Jean-Baptiste seated opposite in his
wheel-chair, grave and still. His wife tried to cheer him up by
inviting some friends, law-officers, questioners, and occasionally
magistrates. It was not unknown for two or three persons of
quality to come and sit at the executioner's table, thus demonstrating their tolerance and broadness of mind, in keeping with
the age of Voltaire and Rousseau. One of this small group
was Monsieur de Lally-Tollendal, who had not forgotten Jean-
Baptiste's wedding-party and the executioner's restraint. Whenever the Count was on leave in Paris he usually made a point of
visiting Jean-Baptiste, more from compassion than feelings of
friendship.

Lally-Tollendal had gone up in rank; he had commanded a
brigade at the battle of Fontenoy, and been promoted Lieutenant-
General at the beginning of the Seven Years' War. The acquain-
tance of this high-ranking officer was a gratifying honour for
Jean-Baptiste; his name was never mentioned in the Sanson
household without a tremor of pride. When, in 1757, he left for
India with a force of 4,000 men and the title of 'Commander of
the French Settlements in Asia,' all the good wishes of Jean-
Baptiste and Madeleine went with him.

That year, 1757, provided an occasion for this remarkable
Sanson tribe to demonstrate its solidarity.

On January 5th a man named François Damiens stabbed

Louis XV in the courtyard at Versailles, as the King was entering his carriage. Because of the bitter cold, Louis XV was wearing two fur-coats, and these saved his life; the knife only made a flesh wound.

It was the first attempt on the life of the reigning monarch since the assassination of Henri IV by Ravaillac; and the same horrible death-sentence inflicted on that regicide was automatically pronounced on Damiens. On March 26th, 1757, he was con-demned to 'be taken to the Place de Grève and there have his chest, arms, and thighs torn with redhot pincers; his right hand, holding the knife used on the King, burnt off with flaming sulphur; molten lead, boiling oil, burning pitch, wax, and sulphur, poured into the places torn with pincers; and then have his body torn apart by four horses.'

When Charles-Henri read this order he shuddered all over, and told his grandmother he could not do it. Jean-Baptiste and his wife were away from Paris at this time; they had bought a house at Brie-Comte-Robert, near Melun, and had gone to stay there in the hope that the country air would be of some benefit to the paralysed man. Old Marthe took charge of the situation. She thought of her other son, Gabriel, executioner at Rheims — he could take the place of Charles-Henri. But the youngster would have to be present at the execution. He held the office of public executioner in his father's name, and the procurator-general — to whom Marthe had maintained he would always be up to the mark — might consider his absence from the scene an excuse to revoke the interim appointment. The heritage of the Sansons was at stake.

Marthe got her grandson to promise to be present, and then wrote to Gabriel. Although he lived and was executioner at Rheims, he also held an office in Paris — that of 'executioner of the sentences and judgments of the King's Household and of the High Provost of France.' This was a sinecure, for the High Provost of the King's Household never pronounced any sentences; at least, not since the time of Louis XI, and that was going back three centuries. The salary was therefore no more than 3,300 livres a year. But the beneficiary, having nothing to do in Paris, was able to live in the provinces and follow any occupation he wished.

So there was nothing to prevent Gabriel coming to Paris, and acting for his nephew in the latter's presence. Thus there would be two Sansons on the scaffold with Damiens. Old Marthe was a strong-willed woman!

She sent a messenger galloping off to Rheims. The family spirit of solidarity came into play; Gabriel hurried as quickly as he could to Paris, believing himself sufficiently hardened to direct the slow and inhuman execution of Damiens.

First he bought four strong horses, deeming Jean-Baptiste's not good enough for tearing Damiens apart. Gabriel paid 432 *livres* for them.

Then he went to see the procurator-general and naively asked him for the name and address of a torturer. 'Because, you see,' he said, 'I supervise and give the orders. But it's not me who uses the pincers, nor pours the molten lead, pitch, and sulphur into the wounds.'

'The address of a torturer?' bellowed the procurator. 'Go and consult the archives and see how a person condemned for lèse-majesté is torn with pincers! It's the public executioner himself who has to do it! He in person, you hear, since it's for an attack on the King. You are taking the place of your nephew, who takes his father's place. That makes you the master-executioner in this instance, and you'll use the pincers yourself!'

Gabriel went white. 'Monsieur le Procureur, you can't mean it! I'd never have the heart to carry out such an operation!'

The magistrate retorted by calling him a coward. Gabriel, in a panic, spoke of giving up his office. What was demanded was beyond him. 'Besides,' he added, 'you'll never find a public executioner who'd agree to do it. An assistant, perhaps — provided he was well paid.'

The procurator-general thought a moment; no doubt he was of the same opinion. Nevertheless, the sentence pronounced had to be inflicted! So, washing his hands of the problem, the magistrate ended by saying, 'Find someone, or I'll dismiss your nephew, and his father at the same time!'

The situation was taking a bad turn for the Sansons.

During the fortnight between this interview and the date fixed for Damiens's execution, the whole Sanson tribe tried to find one of its assistants who would consent to do the horrible job, but all refused; and approaches were made to various prison officials. Eventually a man was found, an elderly, retired 'questioner' by the name of Soubise. He was the son and grandson of 'questioners', and could remember his grandfather talking about the execution of Ravaillac, in which the grandfather had taken part when a young man. Just as there is honour among thieves, Soubise agreed to help out the Sansons by undertaking the pincer part of the sentence himself. Ah, Damiens had no idea of the trouble he was causing so many honest people! And that was not all . . .

At five on Monday morning, March 28th, the date of the execution, Gabriel and Charles-Henri were ready in their traditional costume — blue breeches, red jacket with a gibbet and a ladder embroidered in black. *Monsieur de Paris* and *Monsieur de Rheims* climbed into the cart, each wearing a pinkish two-cornered hat and with a sword at his side. The cart was drawn by two horses, and the four to pull Damiens apart followed behind. Fifteen assistants went with the two master-executioners, each wearing a leather apron.

Charles-Henri and his uncle were present at the Conciergerie when Damiens was put to the question. He revealed no names of accomplices, for he had none; he had acted alone, in a moment of frenzy. The wretched man was tortured for two hours, all the same. At the end, his stomach distended by water, his arms pulled out of their sockets by the strappado, and his ankles broken by the iron boot, he could neither stand nor make any motion. He was put into a leather sack and the top tied round his neck, then some of Charles-Henri's assistants carried him into the Sainte Chapelle and placed him on a bench. There he was left for some hours, with a priest.

Charles-Henri and Gabriel agreed that the former would wait to bring Damiens to the Place de Grève in the middle of the afternoon, while the latter would go and see how the preparations for the execution were progressing. Each kept half the assistants with him.

When Gabriel reached the Hôtel de Ville with his four horses the crowds were beginning to gather in the square, for the exact time of the execution was not known. In the middle, soldiers were lined up round two scaffolds that had been erected during the night by the Parlement's carpenter. This man was independent of the public executioner, although doing work for him. The position was an hereditary one too, by custom rather than right, and was worth almost as much as the office of executioner. One scaffold was tall and wide, for the first part of the sentence to be carried out; and the other was low and much smaller, for the final destruction.

Gabriel saw Soubise was already on the taller scaffold. But he was tottering about, singing and making rude remarks. Regretting his promise to apply the torture, the old man had drunk glass after glass to keep up his courage.

An anxious thought came to Gabriel, and he asked Soubise where he had put the lead and the sulphur, the pitch and the oil. But the drunken man had forgotten to buy them. Gabriel got into a panic and started cursing him; Soubise only burst out laughing. The crowd began to take sides and shout ribald jests. In the middle of all this, the lieutenant of police and then the procurator-general arrived. When the latter discovered the cause of the uproar he snapped at Gabriel:

'It's high time you thought about the preparations! You've neglected your duties — I'm awarding you fifteen days in the dungeons. But now go back to the Conciergerie, and bring the condemned man here. Send me your nephew. I've more confidence in him than in you — he'll do the burning off of the hand and the tearing with pincers!'

'And you lot,' he ordered the executioner's assistants, 'hurry off to the ironmongers' and the grocers' around here, and bring back some lead, sulphur, wax, and pitch! Go on, hurry!'

Gabriel and the assistants did as they were told. But men from the crowd followed the assistants into the shops and prevented anything being sold to them. The lieutenant and his constables had to be sent to force the tradesmen to part with their goods 'in the name of the King'.

This King's acceptance of the Parlement's horrible sentence for an ineffective knife-thrust was deplored by all the people. But the masses were unaware that Louis XV had said of Damiens, 'I do not wish him to die painfully.' The monarchy itself, however, had been attacked by Damiens; and that, far more than harm done to the King's person, required him to die in atrocious suffering. That was what his judges thought, anyway.

Damiens was taken to the Place de Grève at about four in the afternoon. Crowds lined the way, and prayed for him as he passed. In the packed square there were people at every window and even on the roofs. When Gabriel Sanson saw these massed crowds which seemed likely to create trouble at the slightest incident, his courage returned. He aimed a kick at Soubise, who was sleeping off his wine. And to Charles-Henri, who was trembling at having to carry out the procurator's orders, Gabriel hissed, 'Let me get on with it.' The high official and the judges had disappeared inside the Hôtel de Ville. 'He's gone off, away from it all,' Gabriel added.

Damiens was hauled upon the large scaffold. The assistants pulled him out of the sack, while the vicar from nearby St. Paul's said the prayer for the dying. He was tied to a chair, and then his right arm was fixed to a plank with his hand extending beyond it. In accordance with the sentence, Gabriel thrust the knife used on the King into Damiens's hand, bent his fingers round it, and tied them to it. Both he and the condemned man were coughing from the acrid sulphur fumes pouring out of the brazier.

'Courage!' murmured Gabriel, as much for himself as for Damiens.

He drew the flaming brazier up to the guilty hand. Damiens yelled with pain and twisted about in his bonds. Three minutes later, his hand was no more. The sulphur burns prevented the stump from bleeding. Damiens looked at it, his jaws clacking, seemingly surprised at such speediness. As for Gabriel, he staggered back with the brazier, his face all livid and his eyes dilated.

Charles-Henri guessed his uncle had had enough and was near collapse. He took the initiative. 'Legris!' he called to one of the assistants. 'A hundred *livres* for you if you carry on.'

Legris agreed. Other assistants laid Damiens on the floorboards and took off his clothes. Legris, not without some hesitation, drew the long pincers from the brazier and then timidly passed the red-hot ends to and fro above the bare chest, unable to force himself to apply them.

'I said a hundred *livres!*' cried Charles-Henri.

The assistant started to tear off strips of flesh from the chest, arms, and thighs of his victim. Another assistant poured molten lead or burning pitch into the wounds. The martyred man foamed at the mouth, and his eyes almost started from his head. In the end, he lost consciousness.

When he came to, he was stretched out on the smaller scaffold with each of his limbs attached to a rope drawn by a horse. Charles-Henri gave a signal, and the four horses set off in different directions. The cries of the crowd drowned those of Damiens. His limbs, though disjointed and out of their sockets, still held to the trunk. Three times the horses were spurred on with whip and shouts; the vicar of St. Paul's fainted, Gabriel turned away, but Damiens still held together.

Finally, Charles-Henri had to send to the judges for permission to cut the main sinews. At seventeen, he proved himself a callous master.

When Damiens was at last dead it was seen that his hair had turned white during the afternoon.

On that day, March 28th, 1757, the French Revolution began in the hearts of many. By not pardoning Damiens, Louis XV had condemned his grandson, the future Louis XVI.

Gabriel Sanson never got over that clumsy butchery. He gave up his office at Rheims in favour of his son, under the same — and compulsory — conditions as had enabled Charles-Henri to take his father's place. Gabriel offered his nephew his office of 'executioner of the sentences passed by the Grand Provost of France,' in exchange for a pension of 2,400 *livres* a year. Charles-

Henri agreed to the arrangement, and so became the one and only public executioner in Paris. At seventeen years of age!

It was a great achievement in the eyes of old Marthe. The eldest of her grandsons, her favourite and in a way her pupil, had in fact reached the position of head of the family. Now she could be sure the Sanson heritage would not pass into other hands, and the ruthless grandmother at last took things easy. She spent long days sitting in an armchair, some embroidery always between her fingers; the only exception was when Jean-Baptiste and Madeleine came up from Brie-Comte-Robert to stay for a time in Paris. Then the aged mother claimed from her daughter-in-law the pleasure of pushing Jean-Baptiste in his wheel-chair from one room to another.

Not until the day of her death, much later, did she cede her place in the family to her daughter-in-law. Poor Marthe! Death was no longer of any consequence to her, for she had saved that family from sinking into oblivion, and seen its members take their rightful places in the world.

There was no crowd at her funeral. She had been feared and respected, perhaps admired; but never loved. The service was held in St. Laurent's, and then she was laid to rest beside her husband, her sister, and the other Sansons.

Jean-Baptiste, still paralysed, and his wife now never left Brie-Comte-Robert. Gabriel was living in Rheims with his wife and son. In the capital, *Monsieur de Paris* ruled over the family house and his assistants. He had grown tall and strong, like his Abbeville ancestor; and, like him too, called himself the Chevalier de Longval. He had his grandmother's energy and tenacity of purpose. Although his education was fairly wide for the times and he expressed himself well, his spelling was weak. He had become a good musician, even a talented one, playing the violin and the violoncello; his favourite composer was Gluck. It all helped to take his mind off the executions.

He liked dressing up to the nines. Blue was the colour he preferred for his best clothes; with a sword at his side, he was able to delude himself. His pretensions and elegance eventually aroused criticism in high places, and the procurator-general was told to restrain him. He summoned Charles-Henri and, with the excuse that blue was the colour of noble blood, forbade him to wear it. So *Monsieur de Paris* dressed in green and had a new cut given to his clothes. A courtier at Versailles, the Marquis de Letorières, by inverted snobbism set a new mode through imitating him; and before long, all fashionable men were dressing *à la Sanson*.

Charles-Henri often went out shooting. In those times, even the owner of a wood or fields was not allowed to shoot over his own property unless he was of noble descent. But no doubt one or other of the earlier Charles Sansons had obtained exemption from the law forbidding commoners to shoot over anyone's land, by claiming to be — rightly or wrongly — seigneur de Longval. In any case, *Monsieur de Paris* benefited physically and morally from long hours with his gun in the open countryside. The fresh air and exercise was good for his health, and the practice of a sport denied to commoners made him feel superior to those who despised his station in life.

Returning one evening from a day's shooting, his bag safely stowed away in the boot of a post-chaise that he had hired, he called to the postillions to stop at an inn just outside Paris. He was about to sit down at one of the tables when a young Marquise who was dining alone, noticing his elegance of dress, sent him a message by the innkeeper asking him to keep her company. She was returning to Paris from her country estate, and had decided to stay overnight at the inn.

Charles-Henri was fond of women, and was only too happy to spend an hour in such agreeable company. The two enjoyed their meal together and were quite convivial by the end of it. The Marquise naturally asked her guest his name and situation. 'I am the Chevalier de Longval, an officer of the Paris Parlement,' he boldly replied.

She made out she was frightened to go through the long corridors and up to her bedroom by herself, so like a gallant gentleman Charles-Henri offered to accompany her. A desire to follow the affair further came over him. He had the impression that the lady would offer little resistance; the good food and wines had gone to her head. But he had an execution to carry out the following morning; a night of love-making would delay his return to Paris, and might weaken his nerve. He hesitated between duty and pleasure. Suddenly he made up his mind, and called for his post-chaise to be brought round. The young woman's face fell, so he took her by the arm and led her upstairs. She smiled, hopeful again. When they reached the door of her room, he hesitated once more; then went in. Changing his mind, he kissed the hand of the expectant woman and hurriedly took his leave, wishing her a good-night.

The indignant Marquise heard him go out of the inn, and then the sound of his horses setting off. Angrily she went downstairs again, not quite knowing why, and found a gentleman there who was newly arrived.

'Madam, one comes across peculiar people at this inn!' he exclaimed. 'Do you know who the young man is who's just left?'

'He's a . . . an officer,' she stammered. 'The Chevalier de . . . de . . .'

'The public executioner, Madam! I'm sure I'm not mistaken. I've seen him in the Place de Grève on several occasions!'

The disillusioned Marquise groped for a chair. For a moment or two she was struck silent by shock and disgust. Then she called the innkeeper and asked for a bowl of water to wash her hands.

In Paris she consulted an advocate, and in her name he put a request before the Parlement that Sanson should make her a public apology with a rope round his neck; and that in future public executioners should always wear a distinctive sign on their clothes.

Charles-Henri was summoned to appear, but was unable to find any advocate who would agree to defend him. So he prepared his defence himself, and spoke for more than an hour in reply to the advocate who claimed he had committed a crime by sitting at table with the Marquise. He shrewdly drew a connection between his functions and those of the magistrates.

'My acts are but a consequence of your orders,' he said to them. 'If there is anything reprehensible about my office then it is attributable to you, since in the eyes of the law the person who gives orders for a crime is more guilty than the one who carries it out, and so is liable to be similarly classed.'

Extending this theme, Charles-Henri maintained that executioners, like magistrates, protected the public. Without them, 'the whole realm would be infested with brigands.'

He went on to make a comparison with professional soldiers. 'Ask a soldier what his profession is and he'll reply, as I do, that he's a slayer of men. But that has never made people think of avoiding his company, and nobody considers it a dishonour to eat with him! And who does this soldier kill? Innocent people, people who are only doing their duty. Poor orphans and sorrowing widows weep because of him. While I, in the exercise of my functions, respect the innocent and only deal out death to the guilty; I only purge society of the villains disturbing its peace.'

Why then should the public differentiate between 'those defending the State abroad and the one protecting it at home'? By praising the deeds of the army, the amateur advocate lauded by inference his own office and his forefathers. Referring back to the father of Pierre Jouenne, his voice rolled out: 'I have the honour of being the sixth of my family to hold this office, transmitted from father to son. And if an hereditary title of nobility were attached to it, as ought to be the case, I could very likely claim precedence over Madame la Marquise!'

Her advocate retorted by casting scorn upon Sanson's pretensions. 'A nobleman,' he pointed out, 'knows how to use a sword in a different manner.'

Charles-Henri replied to this allusion to duellists by calling them assassins. 'And yet,' he exclaimed, 'the freakish customs of the times treat them as gallant men! Their victim is often guiltless, loyal, and worthy of respect, while mine is always a contemptible person.'

He ended by saying: 'It is asked that I should beg Madame la Marquise's pardon, and that I should wear a distinctive sign on my own clothes. Well, gentlemen, I do not at all seek your indulgence, but I expect everything from your justness!'

The magistrates retired to consider their verdict. After a few minutes that seemed years to Sanson, they returned to announce that 'the papers in the case would remain on the table'. In other words, the application of the Marquise was dismissed.

This triumph increased Charles-Henri's opinion of himself. He received the congratulations of all the family and of the few friends outside the confraternity. Among the latter was a Franciscan monk in holy orders, Brother Ange Gomard, vicar of Picpus.

Charles-Henri's father had known him in the days before being struck down by paralysis. The *abbé* Gomard had been nominated to succeed lay theologians from the Sorbonne in giving last consolation to the condemned, and always had a hard struggle between his duties to the dying and his terror at their agony. One day he had fainted, and Jean-Baptiste's assistants carried him to the Sanson house. The executioner attended to him and kept him there till the following day. As a result, the *abbé* became friendly with Jean-Baptiste, and subsequently with his sons.

Every Friday he was the chief guest at the Sanson table, and gradually told his hosts the story of his life. His youth had been stormy and passionate, and to put an end to it he had entered a monastery. He often spoke of a niece — at least, that was what he called her — whom he adored and whose loose way of living was driving him distracted. His accounts of her morals were as gloomy as his descriptions of her physical attractions were enthusiastic; to such a point that Charles-Henri decided to go and lecture her, in her uncle's name, though really in the hope of savouring the young lady's charms himself. He knew from the *abbé* that she lived in the rue du Bac and had a maidservant. Her money came from a gallant named Jean du Barry, who was talking of marrying her.

Many accounts have been hashed up about a love-affair between Charles-Henri Sanson and the young woman who became the celebrated Madame du Barry. But although he knew her well in her early days, it is impossible to confirm that Charles-Henri preceded Louis XV in her favours. Though she was undoubtedly lavish with them.

In any case, Charles-Henri was getting tired of running after women and his mind was turning towards marriage. The idea of an alliance with the daughter or sister of another executioner did not appeal to him. He wanted a wife from any milieu but that, and sought her among humble folk who might be blinded by his wealth.

Whenever he returned from a day's shooting in the country-side to the north of Paris he passed through the little village of Montmartre. It then consisted of a few farmhouses grouped around the church of St. Pierre, on a hillside that grew vegetables for the Paris markets. Charles-Henri often stopped for a rest at the cottage of a peasant named Jugier. Although knowing his name and what he did, Jugier and his wife welcomed Charles-Henri and sometimes offered him a glass of wine and a slice of sausage-meat. They had a daughter, Marie-Anne, who was 32. A maid of that age, in the 18th century, had given up all hope of marriage. Whether she was pretty or not, we do not know; but she pleased Charles-Henri. Used to going straight to the point, by the harshness of his functions and the brevity of his amorous affairs, he spoke directly to the daughter instead of first approaching the parents. Finding her alone one evening, he asked whether she would be too scared to marry the executioner.

'Indeed not,' Marie-Anne replied, as matter-of-fact as he was. 'I'd willingly marry you if I weren't six years your elder. You'll still be a young man when I'm almost an old woman. The difference in age seems to me a more serious obstacle than the general prejudice against your occupation!'

He laughed. Then, becoming serious, he said, 'It's really me who's the elder. Your rustic activities haven't aged you as much as mine have. Be my wife, the woman of my heart first, and then a sort of elder sister consoling my miseries, if that's really how you see it.'

She accepted him, and the two were married at the parish church of Montmartre on January 20th, 1765.

The new Madame Sanson showed herself to be as authoritative as old Marthe had been, but her character was tempered by a sweet disposition that soon gained her the affection of all the

Sanson family. Her tenderness was often needed. Less than eighteen months after her wedding all Marie-Anne's love and consoling care were called upon, when her husband and father-in-law were stricken by one of the most frightful and dramatic episodes in the history of the Sansons — which is certainly not lacking in them.

Since his departure for India in 1757, the Comte de Lally-Tollendal had sent no news to Jean-Baptiste. Although a noble-man was not ashamed to call at the executioner's house, he did not feel obliged to write to him. But the Sanson family knew, through rumours and popular accounts, of his battles against the British in India. His bravery was well-known, but as an ageing commander he showed a lack of adaptability which prevented him making the best use of his victories. He lost the support of the rajahs, and was finally besieged in Pondichery and surren-dered to the British. Not long afterwards, India was definitely lost to the French.

Lally-Tollendal was taken to London as a prisoner, and there he learnt that the French were demanding his head. He asked to be released on parole, and went to Paris resolved to meet the attacks on his name. He had become vainer and more choleric than ever, and declined all attempts at conciliation; he constituted himself prisoner in the Bastille and demanded to be brought before a tribunal.

As a soldier, he expected to be judged by soldiers. But instead he was brought before the Paris Parlement, and it was then that he realised his mistake. The judges gave him no hearing, and showed themselves set against him from the start. On May 6th, 1766, they sentenced him to death, 'for having betrayed the interests of the King'. Although the Count was 64, Louis XV refused to pardon him.

Charles-Henri was at home awaiting the order to carry out the sentence when he heard a carriage rumble into the courtyard. Going to the window, he saw it had brought his parents. Jean-Baptiste had had little doubt of the result of the Count's trial, and having heard that the verdict confirmed his fears had come up from Brie-Comte-Robert to keep the promise he had made in jest on his wedding-night. 'If ever fate decreed you to be beheaded,' he had said in substance to Lally-Tollendal, 'I give you my word I'd not need two attempts at it.' Little had he imagined that he would ever be reminded of those bantering words! What a terrible coincidence!

Charles-Henri guessed why his father had come to Paris, and how anguished he must be. But although Jean-Baptiste had recovered the use of his limbs, they were thin and feeble and he could hardly stand. Charles-Henri tried to dissuade him from taking his own place as executioner.

'I don't want him to suffer,' Jean-Baptiste repeated obstinately.

His wife, Madeleine, added her pleas to their son's, and reluctantly he gave way. 'But on one condition,' he said to them. 'That you, Charles-Henri, keep my promise for me. You will take my place, in my presence.'

Charles-Henri, though, had not yet been required to execute noblemen, and so had no experience of using the heavy sword of justice. Three days remained before the date of execution; he spent them in practising on dummies. And he and his father decided to have a new sword made, finer and sturdier than the old one which dated back to the time of Charles Sanson the First. The sword-maker had three attempts before Jean-Baptiste was satisfied with the finished product. 'And besides,' he said to his son, 'I shall be on the scaffold to advise you. My presence will be a support to you.'

The fatal day arrived. When the two Sansons entered the Bastille to take charge of the condemned prisoner they found he had attempted to kill himself — with the compass he had used before his judges, to make a map of his campaigns — and the jailers had bound and gagged him. The wound he had given himself was not serious; but he was in a frenzy, rolling his eyes and shaking his mane of silver hair. Suddenly his gaze fixed itself on the eldest of the two men in red who had entered his cell; the Count had recognised Jean-Baptiste.

'And now it's your affair!' cried the procurator, Pasquier, still visibly affected by the recent scene.

After twelve years in retirement, Jean-Baptiste was no longer hardened; his shock at seeing the Count reduced to the plight of a criminal caused him to sink to his knees in front of him. Then, mastering his weakness, he took advantage of his posture to test the ropes binding the Count. 'They're too tight,' he stuttered. 'Loosen them!'

Charles-Henri gave the order to his assistants. The procurator protested, but Jean-Baptiste recovered and stood firm. 'I'm in charge of him now!' he exclaimed. 'You said so yourself.'

Lally-Tollendal, hearing these words, rewarded the executioner with a look of gratitude, and a tear ran down his tragic old face. The ropes round his legs were undone; but his hands remained tied behind his back, and the gag was not removed.

The rest of the story is like a Greek tragedy. At the Place de Grève, Lally-Tollendal went up the steps of the scaffold supported by the two Sansons. He looked at Jean-Baptiste and seemed to be saying, 'Remember your promise.' But the aged executioner could only pull back his sleeve and show his skinny arm. As he dropped weakly into a chair that an assistant pushed under him, he replied to the mute question: 'At our age, Monsieur le Comte, we no longer know how to kill, only how to die. Here is my son; he will keep the promise made by his father.'

The Count thanked him with a nod of the head. Then he knelt down, and Charles-Henri grasped the sword of justice. The crowd in the square gave its usual collective gasp and shudder, although it was keen on this kind of spectacle.

'Stop!' cried Jean-Baptiste.

He got up from his chair, went over to the kneeling man and snatched away the gag. 'Monsieur le Comte, I am master here. The Parlement refused to let you be heard. Speak now. The people are listening.'

'No,' replied Lally-Tollendal. 'I've spoken too much to men; I shall say a few words to God.'

He murmured a long prayer. Jean-Baptiste sat down again. Then the Count called to Charles-Henri. 'Young man, untie my hands.'

'I'm sorry, but the law requires them to be tied behind your back.'

'What need is there to bind my hands in order to cut off my head? I've seen death on forty battlefields; I shan't make a ridiculous struggle. Untie my hands, I want to give my waistcoat to your father.'

The Count had brought it back from India; it had weaves of golden thread and the buttons were small rubies and diamonds. He could not have known that the executioner had a right to the clothes of his victims. In order to let him believe he was making a real present, Charles-Henri unfastened his hands, helped him take off the waistcoat, and gave it to Jean-Baptiste. The assistants had stepped nearer, ready to intervene if necessary. The crowd was becoming restless, not understanding the cause of the delay.

Having made this legacy, the Count allowed his hands to be tied again. 'And now, strike!' he called.

Charles-Henri raised the sword, whirled it round three times and brought it down on the Count's neck. By some diabolical misfortune, just at that moment his long white hair got loose and slipped down. The blade slid across it and cut into his jaw, breaking several teeth. He fell forward but at once recovered himself, still on his knees, with his cheek hanging open and blood streaming down; he shot a look of terrible reproach at Jean-Baptiste.

The crowd shouted insults at Charles-Henri and started to threaten the executioners and their assistants. Greatly alarmed, the senior assistant pushed his young employer aside, grasped the condemned man by the ears and held him down, then shouted to the other assistants to cut at the neck with the damaged blade. Charles-Henri, his mind in a whirl, let the sword be taken from him. The crowd round the scaffold began to surge forward, giving cries of horror. Jean-Baptiste realised the danger; and suddenly recovering his vigour he dashed forward and snatched the sword from the assistant sawing at the neck. His skinny arms whipped it through the air. Charles-Henri and the others sprang back. Then the head of the Count rolled along the boards, cut clean off. And

Jean-Baptiste, exhausted by the effort and nervous strain, collapsed beside it.

Charles-Henri got his doddering father back to the house. He himself spent an awful, sleepless night. The two wives gave all their care to comforting father and son. A few days later, Jean-Baptiste and Madeleine returned to Brie-Comte-Robert with the firm intention of never leaving their country retreat again.

A month afterwards, Charles-Henri was ordered to behead another nobleman... The Chevalier de La Barre had been disrespectful to a procession, but to punish him for this he was falsely charged with having mutilated a wayside cross, a crime that carried the death penalty. He had been condemned to amputation of his hand and to be burnt at the stake, but this was commuted to death by beheading — because of his age, nineteen.

The scene of it all had been Abbeville — the cradle of the Sanson family. Though why *Monsieur de Paris* should be sent there to carry out the execution remains a mystery. Charles-Henri went in the stage-coach, taking four of his assistants with him. At Abbeville, there was no cart for transporting the condemned man from the prison to the public square; the short journey had to be made on foot. The Chevalier de La Barre walked with firm step, a notice with the single word 'Impious' hanging from his neck.

He refused to kneel and make public repentance outside the porch of the parish church. On the scaffold he asked to be allowed to test the blade with his finger. 'I'm less frightened of death than the thought of suffering,' he said to Charles-Henri. 'Try and be more skilful than with Monsieur de Lally-Tollendal.'

Then he added, quite simply and with the assurance of youth, 'Now, strike with a sure hand.'

'But you must kneel down, Monsieur le Chevalier!'

'Ah no! I'm not a criminal. I shall face death standing!'

The executioner realised it was useless to argue, and that it would only weaken the courage of both of them. He raised the sword and struck at the neck with such force and precision that the severed head remained balancing for a few seconds. It only toppled off when the body collapsed.

A story went the rounds that Sanson had impatiently said to his victim, with grim humour, 'Shake yourself, it's done.'

Jean-Baptiste had another stroke after his return to Brie-Comte-Robert, and then he lost his wife. He, the invalid, had expected to die first, ending his days in the country. But fate decided otherwise.

Only the Sansons living in Paris had attended the funeral of old Marthe, who had been respected but no more. Madeleine's funeral, however, drew the whole family, so great was the affection she had inspired. On horseback or by post-chaise they came hurrying to Paris — *Monsieur de Blois, Monsieur de Tours, Monsieur d'Etampes, Monsieur de Provins, Monsieur de Meaux* . . . the seven sons and their wives, the three daughters and their husbands; uncle Gabriel and his son, the executioner in the province of Champagne; aunt Renée-Anne and her husband, Chrétien Zelle, the executioner at Soissons, and their son, who was his deputy. Never had the church of St. Laurent sheltered so many public executioners beneath its roof at one time; there were fifteen of the Longval tribe, without counting those who did not belong to the family.

After the service, the coffin was lowered into the family vault, making the seventh there. Yet a recent decree of the Parlement, dated May 21st, 1765, had prohibited burials inside churches. Members of the royal family and the upper nobility escaped this measure, taken in the interests of public health; and presumably it did not apply to the families of public executioners either. Nor to their assistants, provided they were related to the executioner; for a few days later a poor relative of Madeleine who had acted as assistant to Charles-Henri was laid to rest in the same vault.

Jean-Baptiste had to return to live at the family house in the rue des Poissonniers, so that his daughter-in-law, Marie-Anne, could look after him. He lingered on for a few more years, dying early in 1778. What a curious existence his had been! If any inscription had been put on the stone covering the family vault, instead of it remaining blank, the following lines might well have been seen:

Jean-Baptiste SANSON
Public executioner at the age of seven
Paralysed from his 35th year onwards
Continued to hold office for the next 25 years
Died aged sixty.

CHAPTER FIVE

Charles-Henri, the great Sanson

'LOUIS, by the Grace of God, King of France and of Navarre, to all who see these present, greetings.' Such was the inevitable opening to the letters of appointment, dated February 1st, 1778, which at last invested Charles-Henri Sanson with the office of public executioner after he had been acting for his father for the previous 24 years. Charles-Henri was then 39, and his wife 45. They had two boys — Henri, born on Christmas Eve, 1767, and Gabriel, two years his junior.

For some little while, Charles-Henri had obliged his elder son to be present at executions, thus preparing him for following in his father's office. The boy was sickened by what he saw; his uncle, Cyr-Charlemagne, said later that 'more than once I felt pity for my nephew's faintness at the executions where I had gone with him, to save him from the final cruelties that Charles-Henri was trying to draw his attention to.'

Being the eldest of Jean-Baptiste's ten sons and daughters, Charles-Henri could have kept the property in the rue des Poissonniers; but he preferred to sell it, to share the price with his brothers and sisters. The house and grounds had cost the first Charles Sanson 6,000 *livres* less than a hundred years earlier. His great-grandson got 100,000 *livres* for the property. The purchasers, Papillon and Riboutté, built on the space, and their names were later given to the two short streets.

Charles-Henri rented a house not far away, in what was the rue Neuve-Saint-Jean, not wishing to leave the district he was used to living in. Though not nearly so large, there were nevertheless stables, a coach-house and sheds, around the entrance courtyard. In a wing of the house giving on to the garden and having a separate entrance, Charles-Henri set up a sort of dispensary with a waiting-room for his clients. For he too, like his father and grandfather, practised healing. His wife, the daughter of market-gardeners, turned the grass and flower-beds into a kitchen-garden and looked after it herself.[1]

The rent that Charles-Henri paid for this house in 1778 is not known; but thirteen years later, when he had become the famous Sanson of the French Revolution, a memorandum that he sent to the procurator-general, Roederer, contained this item: 'For the rent of a house to lodge his family and personnel, to stable his horses and carts and the material needed for his functions, the said house being in a situation from where he can carry out his orders promptly... 4,800 *livres*.'

The family life of Charles-Henri and his wife continued as in their old home. Marie-Anne, who was very pious, led all the household in prayer twice a day. Her husband and children, and the kitchen and scaffold staff, followed her into the main living-room morning and evening, and gave the responses as she knelt at her prie-Dieu, below an ivory crucifix hanging on the wall.

During the eight years from 1778 Charles-Henri performed his functions without anything remarkable occurring. His assistants whipped malefactors and put others in the pillory; branded, hanged, broke on the wheel, and beheaded with the axe. Charles-Henri merely supervised proceedings, as no one of noble birth was sent to him.

But in 1786 he thought for a time that the sword of justice would have to be taken from the scabbard where it had been since the execution of the Chevalier de La Barre. The celebrated 'Affair of the Queen's Necklace' brought a Prince-cardinal, two Counts, a Baron, and a Countess before the magistrates. But their judges were unbelievably lenient towards them, and only the Comtesse de La Mothe was sentenced to be punished by the public executioner; not to be beheaded, but hurt and shamed.

Found guilty of having stolen the necklace, Jeanne de La Mothe-Valois was sentenced 'to be beaten and birched naked,

---

[1]) Houses were not numbered in those days. But later, when the rue Neuve-Saint-Jean became the rue du Château d'Eau, the Sanson house was number 16. A part of the house, the wing that gave on to the garden, is still standing today. It is a dilapidated dwelling in the rue de Lancry, number 20.

having a rope round her neck, and then branded on both shoulders with the letter V (for *voleuse*, thief).'

Charles-Henri was rather puzzled when he read the order. This kind of sentence usually included the number of strokes to be given, and specified that they were to be applied to the back. For lack of such precision in the present sentence, had he to obey it to the letter, strip the Countess naked and apply the birch to all the fleshy parts of her body? He went to the Palais de Justice and asked the chief magistrate, Joly de Fleury, just what was intended by the words 'beaten and birched naked'. There is no record of the reply, except that the magistrate requested Sanson to 'arrange matters to avoid any scene' and to 'reconcile the requirements of humanity with the severity of the sentence'. And to these ends, he was to carry out the sentence at six in the morning, inside the courtyard of the Palais de Justice, to avoid a large crowd being present and seeing the Countess humiliated.

So Charles-Henri, with some of his assistants, returned soon after daybreak on June 21st to collect the prisoner from the Conciergerie. Behind the large wrought-iron gates of the Palais de Justice the carpenters were just finishing erecting a wooden platform with a smaller one, about the size of a single divan, set upon it. Madame de La Mothe was still asleep in her cell. She was a young woman, about 30, a descendant of an illegitimate son of Henri 11 — which was why she took the royal name of Valois. Sanson sent the jailer's wife to rouse her, by saying that her advocate was waiting.

The Countess put on a silk deshabillé with brown-and-white stripes, tied up her hair and slipped a lace bonnet on. When she appeared, two of Sanson's assistants seized her by the arms.

'What do you think you're doing?' she cried.

'Taking you to hear your sentence,' replied Charles-Henri.

The Countess began to tremble; she had not yet been informed of the verdict. 'All right, come on, then,' she said, regaining control of herself. With a twist, she freed her arms and started to walk disdainfully ahead, like a great lady — which she was, in spite of the theft.

When they reached the room where the magistrates were

waiting, she refused to kneel while the sentence was read to her. Sanson, thinking of other afflictions awaiting her, refrained from forcing her to obey. As soon as she heard the pronouncement of her guilt, Madame de La Mothe started to exclaim; when the sentence was read she lost her haughty attitude, and with a shriek cast herself on the floor. She threw herself about so much that Charles-Henri and his assistants had difficulty in holding her.

'Do your duty!' the procurator cried to the executioner, giving up reading the sentence to the end.

The Countess, thinking she was about to be stripped and beaten there and then, started to struggle wildly. She had to be tied before it was possible to take her out and round to the courtyard. When she was lifted on to the platform, and saw the faces at the windows and the people peering through the gates she started to shriek again, and suddenly shouted, 'If someone with the blood of the Valois in her veins is treated like this, what kind of fate is in store for the Bourbons?'

She was thus, unknowingly, predicting the future . . .

When untied by Sanson's assistants she at once wrenched herself free of them and ran to the edge of the platform. They caught her again, and she spat and scratched, and gave one such a clout that he almost toppled down to the cobbles, ten feet below.

Fortunately for the application of the sentence, she had on only a shift beneath her deshabillé. Sanson's assistants managed to tear them off her, bit by bit, and then kept her held face down on the wooden divan. As she was of noble birth, Sanson had to administer the birching himself. Brandishing the bundle of long, flexible twigs, and incited by the long struggle, he laid on the birch with vigour and perhaps with the unconscious desire of taking revenge on the flesh of an aristocrat for all the humiliations imposed on the race of executioners.

When he stopped, the platform looked as if it had been the scene of a battle. The executioner and his assistants were wiping the sweat from their brows; the Countess was crying and sobbing, half-lying on the low bench.

'It's my own fault that I've suffered this shame,' she suddenly exclaimed between her tears. 'I had only to say a word, and I'd have been hanged!'

But there she was mistaken; women of her rank were beheaded.

Charles-Henri took advantage of the comparative calm to start branding her. He drew the iron from the glowing brazier and roughly applied it to her shoulder. Madame de La Mothe, taken unawares, gave a howl of pain. She did not know of this part of the sentence, having by her behaviour cut short the reading of it. She fell against the one assistant still holding her and bit his hand so fiercely that a strip of skin came away.

The frightful struggle began again. They got her to her knees, and Charles-Henri was quickly bringing down the branding-iron when she suddenly twisted round; he was unable to stop himself, and the mark of the shameful letter was burnt upon her breast.

Sanson's assistants usually did the branding, on the backs of harlots and of men condemned to the galleys; it was the first time Charles-Henri had branded anyone himself, and a painful impression was left in his mind. A similar shameful mark was carried by him too; not on his skin, but on his jacket of office and in the form of a gibbet and a ladder. He asked permission to remove these ignominious badges, and it was granted. From then on, he could dress as he liked when he carried out his functions.

Some while later, he was talking with a magistrate who, without seeing any harm in it, called him *Monsieur le Bourreau* — *bourreau* being the common word for a public executioner, and meaning hangman and brute.

'No!' objected Sanson. 'I'm the executioner of criminal sentences.' That was his proper title, the other was derogatory and insulting, so he considered. And he petitioned the King for the use of the term *bourreau* to be forbidden all over France.

The Normandy Parlement had issued a decree, in 1661, which imposed a fine of 50 *livres* on anyone calling the public executioner a *bourreau*. Half the amount of the fine went to the *bour . . .* er, to the public executioner. In 1781 this same provincial

Parlement had increased the fine to a hundred *livres*, which benefited a certain Jouenne, a remote relative of Charles-Henri Sanson. By referring to these decrees, Charles-Henri obtained the application of a similar measure to the whole of France. He had the pleasure of reading: 'By decree dated January 12th, 1787, His Majesty expressly forbids and prohibits the term *bourreau* being applied to executioners of criminal sentences.'

There was no mention of any fine. But Sanson was sufficiently satisfied with the interdiction.

Public opinion was growing against the barbarous practice of breaking condemned prisoners on the wheel. It had been introduced from Germany early in the 16th century. There were then 115 different crimes against civil and ecclesiastical laws which were punishable by death. But whereas murderers were hanged, thieves and robbers were broken on the wheel. No doubt the authorities considered that property was more sacred than human life. However, when the Age of Reason began to shine, still somewhat dimly, judges sentenced assassins to the wheel as well as robbers. Equality for all, but equality in barbarism. The gibbet and the block being used less and less, Sanson was the living symbol of the frightful death penalty in the eyes of the awakened and enlightened crowds.

The people showed they were indeed roused, and Charles-Henri had a narrow escape from their fury, one August day in 1788, at Versailles. He had received orders to break a parricide named Louschart on the wheel. Louschart had, in fact, killed his father by accident. The two held strongly opposed political beliefs, the father — a blacksmith to the Court — being an ardent royalist and reactionary, the son an enthusiast for the revolutionary spirit that was abroad. The fatal quarrel, though, had broken out over a young cousin, an orphan girl to whom the blacksmith had given a home. The son wanted to marry her; but the father, a widower, thought that a good way to punish him for his revolutionary ideas was to marry the girl himself. The son protested, the father seized a hammer to threaten him; young Louschart wrenched it away and, not wanting to fight his own father, walked to the door, tossing the hammer over his shoulder. Unknown to him, it caught his father on the head and killed him outright. Young Louschart only knew of this when arrested in a street at Sèvres, where he was wandering about and lamenting his lost love.

Louschart was tried at Versailles, and Sanson had to go there to carry out the sentence. But in the meantime a local linen-draper named Lecointre — who later became a member of the Convention — had whipped up the population, and a hostile crowd followed Sanson's cart when it left the prison with the condemned man. In the Place St. Louis, where the scaffold had been erected, a seething mass of people threatened at any moment to break through the guard.

Louschart, mounting the steps of the scaffold with Sanson, begged him to do the job swiftly. The *retentum* had been granted at the last moment by the King. 'Since I've got to die,' said Louschart, 'there's no point in making me suffer too long.'

'If there's anyone here who's near his last hour,' Sanson replied, seeing fists being shaken at him, 'it certainly isn't you!'

The leader of the mob shouted a signal, and a crowd of men surged forward, thrust aside the guard and dashed towards the scaffold. A man dressed like a blacksmith was first up the steps, followed by a group of excited workmates. In a minute, Louschart had been released and carried away shoulder-high. Sanson was standing to one side, ready to defend himself.

'Leave the hangman alone!' the blacksmith shouted, then turned to Sanson and snapped, 'It's not you we want, Charlie, but your tools. In future, when you're sent a customer, kill him without torturing him!'

Sanson's assistants had already fled, and he followed suit. The rioters tore down the scaffold, broke up the wheel and the St. Andrew's cross, and threw all the pieces on the fire prepared for the burning of Louschart's dead body. Then a great bonfire was lit, and the crowd danced round it until all was reduced to ashes.

When Louis XVI was informed of what had occurred he pardoned Louschart and abolished the ancient, barbarous method of execution. Sanson was left with only the rope and the axe.

Fearing other riots, directed against the gibbet and the block, magistrates in general extended their leniency which the progressive ideas of the times had begun to force upon them. This resulted in a considerable decrease in Sanson's income, as he received so much per journey and per head. His basic salary, fixed by the Regent at 16,000 *livres* a year, had only been increased by 1,000 since then. Moreover, the Royal Treasury being in difficulties, it was several years since Sanson had been paid his 17,000 *livres*. And then there were the fees and fiscal expenses to do with his father's estate and the share-out of the inheritance. Altogether, Charles-Henri was running into financial trouble.

He gave credit-notes to his suppliers, and signed postdated drafts to hold off the most pressing of his creditors. Soon he could see the time approaching when his furniture and horses would be seized to pay his debts. Even the threat of imprisonment hung over him. There seemed only one possible way out of his troubles — an appeal to the royal favour. He had a plea drawn up, and requested the Parlement to present it to the King. A week later he was summoned to Versailles.

On April 19th, 1789, Charles-Henri Sanson entered the château and was conducted to have audience of the King. When Sanson was shown into the room, Louis XVI was standing in the bay of a window and looking out at the gardens. He remained with his back turned throughout the interview, only glancing at Sanson towards the end of it, thus enabling the executioner to describe later to his family how the King was dressed: 'A jacket of lilac-coloured taffeta, embroidered in gold, with the star of the Order of the St. Esprit shining on it; short breeches, silk stockings, and buckle-shoes. A lace frill was round his loose cravat, which revealed his prominent neck muscles.'

Through perverted professional curiosity, Charles-Henri always looked at the neck of people he met. If he had known that neck would later . . .!

The story was put about by malicious gossip, years afterwards, that when describing this audience of the King a short time later Sanson had said: 'I liked the look of his face — he has a head that keeps coming back to me.'

Without turning away from the window, Louis XVI said to Sanson: 'You have made a request for some sums that would appear to be owing to you. Your accounts will be checked, I promise you. Unfortunately, the State coffers are hardly full just now, and you are asking for 136,000 *livres*, which is a considerable amount.'

'Sire,' replied Sanson, 'I thank Your Majesty for his kindness towards me. But I humbly beg him to allow me to point out that my debts have increased so greatly that my creditors are becoming impatient, talk of suing me and so threaten my liberty. If they get me thrown into prison I should no longer be able to carry out my functions in the service of Your Majesty.'

At these last words, which could have been considered impudent, Louis XVI gave a little shudder. Turning his head, he glanced at the speaker. Sanson was some way off, just inside the doorway, and was bowed so low that his face could not be seen, only his wig.

'Monsieur de Villedeuil,' the King said to the gentleman of the Household who had brought Sanson. 'Take a pen and write this:

'By order of the King,

His Majesty, wishing to give the sieur Charles-Henri Sanson the means of going about his affairs, has accorded him safe-conduct for three months, during which time His Majesty forbids his creditors to take any steps against him; forbids any bailiff, constable, or other person to arrest or molest him; any jailer or prison-turnkey to admit him, under pain of disobedience, of dismissal from their office, and payment of expenses, damages and interest.'

Louis XVI signed the order and returned to his window. Sanson bowed to the ground, and pocketed the safe-conduct which solved none of his financial problems. For three months he was as free and light as his purse. It was a neat and easy method, to an absolute monarch, for shaking off a creditor...

As the public executioner was making his way to the staircase he saw two ladies approaching and everyone bowing as they passed. He did the same, not knowing he had set eyes on Marie-

Antoinette and her sister-in-law Elisabeth — two women of whom he could equally have said, 'They have heads that keep coming back to me.'

Less than three months after Sanson's audience of the King, the Bastille fell. After that, events moved swiftly. In October, the Paris mob plodded out to Versailles and forced the King and Queen to return with them to Paris and take up residence at the Tuileries.

On December 24th the Constituant Assembly was debating clauses in the electoral laws that debarred certain categories of people from voting, and several members proposed that the 60 public executioners in the country should be included among these categories. When put to the vote, however, the motion was rejected.

Charles-Henri felt nevertheless that his position was in danger. He considered he was a part of the old order of things, and was likely to be condemned along with it. Moreover, the abolition of the death penalty was a subject being much discussed. The champion of this reform was a journalist named Elysée Loustalot. In a popular news-sheet called *Révolutions de Paris* he wrote: 'It's said that the death penalty is necessary to prevent the criminal committing another offence. Then give him hard labour, make him do something useful! Look at all the public work that is degrading for a citizen, and at which only criminals should be employed!'

Loustalot added that the death penalty had never stopped crime from being committed. Other journalists wielded their pens against 'that barbarous custom, unworthy of the French people'. In the gardens of the Palais Royal, public speakers stood on chairs and declaimed against it.

For some time Sanson had feared that the end of absolute monarchy would entail the end of old methods of repression. So he thought he would be protecting his own future by helping to bolster up the aristocratic regime. He gave over a room of his house to a clandestine printing-press. He had no part in its operations, and charged rent for the room, but from it pamphlets went out daily to be distributed in Paris and the provinces, carrying anti-democratic propaganda and attacking the Assembly.

The police got wind of it, and one morning raided Sanson's house. He was arrested and taken to the Châtelet prison. Decidedly, things were all against him.

The Revolutionary press got hold of the story, and several of the popular papers gave exaggerated accounts; Sanson was denounced and his past raked up. A member of the Assembly, Gorsas, attacked him in the *Courrier de Paris*.

Charles-Henri succeeded in convincing the police that he was unaware of the nature of the broadsheets printed at his house. He let the room, he said, to get a little money to give to the poor of the parish. He was released provisionally, and went to consult an advocate, Maton de La Varenne.

'The best means of defence,' the latter told him, 'is attack.' And proposed that he should sue Gorsas, who had written in the *Courrier de Paris* that 'the public executioner had in his house the printing-press that produced all those abominable lampoons which were distributed in the provinces to excite the people to revolt and murder . . .'

Gorsas did not appear in court, and Sanson's advocate won the case. The journalist was ordered to publish a retraction in his own paper, to pay the cost of posting up 300 copies of the verdict, and to pay a hundred *livres* in damages to Sanson — who agreed to give them to the poor of his parish.

The defendant got his own back by calling the public executioner *bourreau* four times in a commentary on the case that he printed in his paper before making the retraction. But Sanson had the last word, three-and-a-half years later, when he carted Gorsas to the guillotine!

Such a final meeting with Sanson was not foreseen by Camille Desmoulins either, when he wrote in his paper, *Révolutions de France et de Brabant*, 'I call a spade a spade, and Sanson the *bourreau*.' This made Charles-Henri want to sue the whole lot of these scribblers, but Maton de La Varenne managed to dissuade him, putting forward his own idea: to obtain an amendment to the law voted on December 24th, 1789, concerning elegibility to appear on the electoral rolls. The advocate wanted it definitely stated that 'The Assembly includes public executioners in the number of citizens,' and for the clause to be added, 'It orders the enforcement of the various decrees forbidding the name *bourreau* to be applied to executioners.'

Sanson agreed, and Maton de La Varenne drew up a long memorandum that he sent to the President of the Assembly. It referred to 'the just grievancies of a group of men on whom blind prejudice has put a mark of infamy,' and went on to request the Assembly to denounce the stupid tales told about them. 'The people must be told that public executioners take their oath of office standing, and not with their head in the dust; that they are accepted only after enquiry into their habits and conduct, with a certificate that they are good Catholics.' Finally, it recalled that the term *bourreau* was forbidden by various decrees, and gave the dates.

The Assembly paid little attention to this memorandum, though it was communicated to the press. Most of the papers printed the main passages; even Marat's sheet, in which he admitted — not without irony — that he had been unable to read it 'without feeling touched'. But it all bore some fruit, influencing public opinion to the extent that Charles-Henri was able to enrol in the National Guard, which was a reserve force of armed citizens.

This new duty did not prevent Sanson from continuing to perform the functions of his office, which recent laws had reduced to standing malefactors in the pillory and a single method of applying the death penalty — by hanging. The National Assembly had voted equality for all in this respect too; whether the con-demned was a nobleman or a commoner, he was sent to the gallows. Such was the fate of the brothers Agasse, found guilty of issuing forged notes; and of the Marquis de Favras, accused of plotting against the State — of a mad project to kidnap the King, who was practically a prisoner in the Tuileries.

In spite of the comparative leniency shown to criminals not charged with murder, the courts still sentenced forgers to death.

A couple of centuries earlier they would have been boiled alive. From being plunged into boiling water to being strung up on the gallows, was nevertheless an improvement. It had long been customary, however, for forgers to be given a death sentence; which caused Prud'homme to write in his paper: 'It's *customary...* Cannibals! What do your abominable customs matter? Does the guilty man cease to be a human being, to be your brother?'

A great crowd gathered when the Marquis de Favras was hanged; half the people yelled approval at seeing an aristocrat despatched by a method that had previously been used only on commoners, while the other half raised their voices in protest against a sentence so disproportionate to the offence committed. A few shouts of 'Reprieve!' rose from the crowd when the Marquis mounted the steps of the gallows, led by Charles-Henri.

The latter was wearing his new official dress — a top-hat, slightly convex in shape, like the English fashion of the time, and a frock-coat of dark material, tightly buttoned. The man in red had become the man in black...

Charles-Henri had an unusual sentence to execute when, on March 15th, 1790, an exception was made to the new law in the case of a certain Pierre Curé, found guilty of disrespect to Her Majesty the Queen. He was sentenced 'to make public penitence in front of the main porch of the Church of Paris, being taken there in a tumbril by the public executioner and having a notice on his chest and back with the words, 'Seditionist, disturber of the public peace'; to be stood in the pillory for three days, to be birched naked, branded with the letters GAL on both shoulders, and sent to the *galleys* for life.'

This sentence shows that judges were still protecting Marie-Antoinette. As Pierre Curé had been found guilty of *lèse majesté*, Sanson himself should have birched and branded the man. But he left it to his assistants, and the procurator turned a blind eye. The public executioner had other irons to put in the fire, so to speak, than for the branding of a poor fellow who had shouted, 'The Austrian woman is a whore!'

For Sanson was still trying to get his money, and was co-operating with the invention of a new death-dealing machine...

The new rulers of the State did not pay their officials any better than the old, and Charles-Henri now had his two brothers, an invalid sister, and old uncle Gabriel to look after and keep. Altogether there were 17 persons living at his house in the rue Neuve-Saint-Jean: himself and his wife and their two sons, his two brothers and the sister, 75-year-old uncle Gabriel and his wife, and a staff of eight consisting of a cook, four assistants, and three carters.

His two sons were named Henri and Gabriel, and in 1792 were aged respectively 25 and 23. Both helped their father with his functions as executioner. Charles-Henri's two brothers had been public executioners in the provinces, but were dismissed for some unknown reasons and had come to live with *Monsieur de Paris*. In exchange for their keep they acted as assistants to him, sometimes taking his place as principal when there were several sentences to be executed on the same day in different parts of the city.

Old uncle Gabriel tried to make himself useful in the store-sheds; and Charles-Henri could not forget the support he had given the family at the time of the gruesome Damiens affair. In 1789 Charles-Henri had been unable to continue paying him the pension of 2,400 *livres* — promised in exchange for Gabriel's sinecure, as already mentioned — and had offered a home to his old uncle and aunt. Little is known about his invalid sister, except that she was the widow of the public executioner at Etampes.

Charles-Henri had 17 persons, then, to provide board and lodging for; and the money was not coming in. He addressed a memorandum on the matter to Roederer, the procurator-general, enumerating his difficulties and complaints. He gave the cost, item by item, of the salaries of his assistants and carters, of feeding his staff and his horses, repairs to the carts, the rent of the house, clothing, laundering, and upkeep. The total came to 27,798 *livres* a year. Charles-Henri gave the reasons for the high salaries he had to pay; his spelling and grammar were far from perfect, but the gist of it could be understood — that the class of man he had been used to employing as assistant now found it easier to get other jobs or was joining the army, and only better pay drew them to him. And he concluded by stating how deeply he was in debt, requested the settlement of his overdue accounts, and threatened to resign his office if he did not receive satisfaction.

Apparently he did obtain the money owing to him, as he continued in office and eventually became, with the invention of the guillotine, the head of a new school of executioners; and was called 'the great Sanson' by all the executioners in the provinces.

His principal students at the macabre lessons were his two sons, Henri and Gabriel; the four assistants, Demorets the elder and Demorets the younger, François Le Gros, and Levasseur; and three others, Barré, Fermain, and Colas.

Then there were the executioners who came up from the provinces: Charles-Martin Sanson, executioner at Tours and then at Auxerre, and his son, Louis-Victor, who was executioner at Montpellier; Louis-Cyr-Charlemagne Sanson, executioner at Provins and then at Versailles; Jean-Louis Sanson, executioner at Rheims; Constant Vermeille, executioner at Cambrai; Joseph Heinderech, at Mâcon; Berger, at Carpentras, who assisted a Sanson renowned for his drunkenness; Nicolas-Richard Jouenne, executioner at Caudebec, and Nicolas-Lubin Jouenne, at Melun; Collet de Charmoy, executioner at La Rochelle and later at Amiens, whose sister married Charles-Martin Sanson. The list could be extended, all being closely or distantly related to Charles-Henri, the great Sanson; a total of 34 were initiated in the new method by the best known member of the family. There would have been 60 of them, if the Revolution had not removed the old provincial divisions of France and thereby reduced their numbers. All learnt from *Monsieur de Paris* how to work the guillotine, a machine that in spite of its name was not invented by Doctor Guillotin.

Since the execution of the Marquis de Favras by hanging, the judicial authorities had been trying to find a means of despatching the condemned in a manner that would be swift and painless. A Doctor Guillotin, who had been a member of the Constituent

Assembly and acquired some celebrity there, was given the task of discovering 'a fresh method of beheading'. Away with the axe and the block, something else was needed!

Guillotin plunged into the archives. He came across a sketch made by Albert Dürer in the 16th century showing the Roman dictator, Titus Manlius Torquatus, beheading his own son with a peculiar kind of apparatus; and a similar, slightly-improved model had been used by the executioner at Toulouse for the beheading of Marshal de Montmorency in 1632 — 'an axe held between two blocks of wood, with a cord attached that was pulled when the condemned man's head was on the block, so that the axe fell and separated the head from the body.'

There was also the Maiden, which had been used for a time at Edinburgh in the 16th century. Instead of an aperture in the block, this had a small St. Andrew's cross on which the condemned man, kneeling down, placed his neck; an axe with a heavy weight attached was held upright by a length of cord, which was cut at the fatal moment. But the Maiden had been forsaken after causing some atrocious sufferings.

Guillotin tried to find some way of improving this awkward apparatus, and went to the Sanson house to seek the advice of Charles-Henri. They studied the problem together. Instead of the condemned person kneeling down and poking his head forward, they came to the conclusion he ought to be stretched out on the ground so that the blade would strike the neck with greater force. But then the blade would get dented by contact with the ground or the cobbles, and so could not be used more than once. How were they to solve that problem?

A friend of Sanson's was present at the second meeting. He was a German named Tobias Schmidt, a maker of harpsichords. Charles-Henri, it will be remembered, liked to play the violin in the evenings; and his aunt Renée-Anne, the widow of the executioner at Soissons, Chrétien Zelle, had put the German in touch with him. Chrétien Zelle had been another public executioner fond of music; he used to play the harpsichord at public concerts, and his marriage-certificate gave him as 'musician'. His widow, wishing to please her nephew, brought her husband's friend to meet Charles-Henri — never dreaming that the German musician's imagination would be roused, after an evening with Guillotin, to ... invent the guillotine.

For the sinister machine ought rather to have been named 'the schmidtine'. Sanson and Schmidt often played together at each other's homes, the executioner on the violin and the German at the harpsichord. One evening, after playing a piece by Gluck, Schmidt suddenly exclaimed in his thick accent, 'I've got it! Your doctor vill be pleased!'

Taking a piece of paper, he drew a rough sketch of an instrument destined to make sounds different from those of a spinet. Everything was there — the sliding plank and the aperture, which overcame the inadequacies of the Maiden, and even a cutting-blade shaped like a crescent that took the place of the axe and, to the inventor's mind, would shear the neck more effectively.

Doctor Guillotin was shown the sketch, and approved of it. All three went to see Guédon, the master-carpenter and joiner of the Parlement. He studied the means of constructing such a machine, and made an estimate of the cost:

To timber for the machine, its scaffold and

steps	1,700	*livres*
To the ironwork	600	,,
To three blades (two in reserve)	300	,,
To pulleys and copper grooves	300	,,
To the iron drop-weight (for the blade) . .	300	,,
To rope and rigging	60	,,
To constructing the whole, testing it, and time spent discussing it	1,200	,,
To a small-scale model for demonstrations to prevent accidents	1,200	,,
Total	5,660	*livres*

When this exorbitant estimate reached the public prosecutor, he refused to accept it and advised the Minister for Finance, Clavière, to seek the opinion of 'any other craftsman'. The Assembly decided that the plans and estimates submitted should be examined by Antoine Louis, a surgeon and physician to the King.

Louis did not have long to wait. Schmidt himself offered to construct his machine, in his own workshop, for 824 *livres*. This was a great difference from Guédon's 5,660! In spite of the moderate price, the harpsichord manufacturer did a good stroke of business; for there would be 34 guillotines to supply, one to each of the public executioners in the provinces. Wholesale production called for a wholesale price.

Guillotin, Schmidt, and Sanson went to see Louis together, taking the sketch and estimate. It was on March 2nd, 1792, that they were received at the Tuileries, where the physician to the King had rooms. The château was more like the tomb of the Monarchy, then, and very little like a brilliant royal palace. Instead of a glittering crowd of courtiers there were the gloomy faces of the few last trusty followers and the watchful presence of National Guards.

Antoine Louis was sitting at a table covered with green velvet when the three were shown into his study. While they were talking, a door opened and a gentleman walked in unannounced. When Charles-Henri saw this portly, plainly-dressed person he gave a start, and instinctively moved away into a corner. He had recognised Louis XVI, although the King's haggard expression and prematurely-aged face made him look very different from the young monarch who had given audience to the executioner three years previously.

The physician rose from his chair but did not bow. The King had doubtlessly warned him of his coming incognito. He bent over the table and examined Schmidt's sketch, listening to the explanations given by the physician. The maker of harpsichords kept glancing at the King, puzzled as to who he could be.

'This crescent-shaped blade with the ends pointing downwards,' said Louis XVI slowly, placing his finger on the drawing, 'doesn't seem very practical to me. Do you think a blade of that kind would act equally well on every type of neck? It would be too wide for thin ones, and much too narrow for thick.'

Sanson, hearing this, automatically looked at the King's neck.

It had attracted his attention at Versailles; unusually large and muscular, it exceeded the inside width of the blade drawn by Schmidt. An uneasy feeling came over the executioner; hardly a premonition, but some strange foreboding of the mind. As though struck by a telepathetic thought, Louis XVI turned his head and looked at Sanson. Then, bending towards the physician, he whispered, 'Is that the man?'

The physician nodded. 'Ask him for his opinion,' murmured the King.

'You heard the objection made by *Monsieur*,' the physician said to Sanson. 'What do you think about the shape and size of the blade?'

'Monsieur is quite right. Its present form might lead to difficulties.'

Louis XVI made locks in his leisure time. The vice he used can still be seen at the Carnavalet Museum. In the church of St. Laurent — the same one as where the early Sansons were buried — is a fine sculptured wardrobe presented by Madame du Barry, and its handsome locks were cut and fixed by Louis XVI. With his experience of mechanical instruments, the King considered that a blade with a slanting edge would befit any kind of neck and shear with greater rapidity. If the four listening to him, watching him draw an outline of the blade, could have seen into the future...

Five days after this extraordinary meeting, Antoine Louis presented his report to the Assembly and it was adopted. All that remained was for Schmidt to construct the machine and for Sanson to test it.

It was ready on April 15th and tried out on live sheep, in the courtyard of Schmidt's workshop in the rue de Thionville-au-Musée. Two days later it was tested on five human corpses, at the Bicêtre hospital. Sanson worked the machine in the presence of the governor of the hospital, Doctor Cullerier, Schmidt, Antoine Louis, and of course Guillotin. Three heads were sheared clean from the bodies with the slanting blade suggested by Louis XVI; the crescent blade only cut into the necks of the other two. The King could boast of being right...

When Guillotin gave an account to the National Assembly he had a great success, the members shaking with laughter at some of his remarks and descriptions: 'The condemned man will feel at most a slight chill on his neck.' 'With this machine I can have your head off in a flash and you won't suffer at all.' 'The knife comes down like lightning, the head flies off, blood spurts, the man has ceased to exist.'

Wishing to show that the machine was the work of responsible men, Guillotin mentioned the physician's name much more than the harpsichord maker's. So much so that Louis was regarded as the real inventor, and the machine was immediately called 'the Louison' or 'the Louisette.' No one had yet thought of naming it after Guillotin.

It was inaugurated on April 25th, 1792, when a man named Pelletier was . . . decapitated. He had been found guilty of theft. One journalist reported the execution thus: 'The young Louison was tried out yesterday, and a head was chopped off . . . I have never been able to go near a man who has been hanged, and I must confess I've an even greater repugnance for this method of execution. The preparations make one shudder, and must add to the mental sufferings; as to the physical ones, somebody who was present at the execution told me it was done in the twinkling of an eye. The people seemed to want a return to the old regime, and to be saying to Sanson:

> 'Give me back my wooden gibbet,
> Give me back my gibbet'.'

This was a couplet from a popular song. And it was another song that caused 'the Louison' to be named after Guillotin, a song by some unknown composer who chivvied the doctor for his enthusiastic account to the Assembly. All Paris was soon singing:

> 'Guillotin,
> Physician,
> Politician,
> Found one fine morning
> How inhuman is hanging,
> And unbecoming the Nation.

> So instead,
> From his head
> Came the Machine
> Which will kill us cleanly
> And be known namely
> Guillotine.'

Thus do words get into the dictionary. Through humming the refrain, the Parisians substituted 'the Guillotine' for 'the Louison.'

Sanson worked the machine in the Place de Grève during the next few weeks. Three soldiers guilty of attempted murder followed Pelletier, and then three forgers. The eighth customer, another forger, got caught up in a mass demonstration for the guillotine to be transferred elsewhere. When Sanson brought him — his name was Collot — to the Place de Grève in the cart, the waiting crowd started to jeer at the condemned man and to shout, 'To the Carrousel!'

A man seized the horse by the bridle. 'Charlie!' he cried, 'the Commune wants the Louison set up outside the tyrant's palace, and his toadies and menials to be executed there! You've got to take your machine and your man there right away!'

The people around him took up the cry. 'To the Carrousel!' This was the name of the square outside the gates of the Tuileries palace.

Sanson replied to these demands by stating his orders. But this only increased the tumult, and threats were directed against the executioner. He went across to the Hôtel de Ville to ask for fresh instructions.

While Sanson was in the town hall, the group of agitators succeeded in rousing the support of the whole crowd. A yelling mass of people surrounded the cart, shouting abuse at the condemned man, Collot, who already looked more dead than alive, and they turned the cart round in the direction of the Place du Carrousel. Then they started shaking the scaffold and taking it down, and came to grips with Sanson's assistants, who all made off, except one.

The magistrates watching all this from the windows of the town hall realised the futility of opposing the mob. 'Do what the people want!' they told Sanson.

He pushed his way back through the crowd, announcing that its demands were agreed to; and a hundred people, shouting in triumph, hurriedly completed taking the scaffold to pieces. Sanson had great difficulty in protecting his guillotine from their hands. When all had been taken down, the poles and planks piled into a couple of tumbrils and into Sanson's cart, almost crushing poor Collot, the ragged procession set off, singing and shouting, towards the Tuileries. It had barely a mile to go, but took two hours; the mob led the carts in long detours, and made several halts outside taverns on the way. Sanson's missing assistants were waiting for him by the tall iron gates of the Tuileries, but having drunk many a glass with the *sans-culottes* they were in no state to aid their master. It was getting dark too, and torches had to be lit. Collot, driven half mad by all that had happened, was writhing in his bonds.

'I can't carry out an execution in these conditions!' Sanson shouted at the crowd. 'By the time the scaffold and the machine are erected again, it'll be completely dark. Citizens, I ask you to send to the Commune for permission to put off the execution!'

This was greeted with boos and jeers. 'You're trying to save the enemies of the nation!' a lanky young hooligan in the red bonnet and carmagnole jacket of a revolutionist flung at Sanson. 'You traitor! We'll poke your mug into the lookout-hole of your Louison!'

'My assistants are drunk!' Sanson retorted.

'You can have a thousand assistants for each one of them,' the hothead shouted back. 'There isn't a single patriot who wouldn't be proud to spill the blood of enemies of the people! Ain't that so, you lot?'

The crowd yelled its support, and started to put the scaffold up, more or less correctly, under the direction of a master-joiner. Then Charles-Henri and his one sober assistant erected the guillotine.

'And now,' he cried, 'where are these assistants you offered me? I need three.'

The crowd fell suddenly silent.

'Well, I'm waiting for them!'

Collot, lifted up to the scaffold by Sanson's assistant, began to shout, 'I don't want to die!'

The mob lost its cruelty at the sight. In the hush that had come over it, Sanson was heard calling to the lanky youngster in the red bonnet. 'Citizen, you said I'd have a thousand assistants. Set an example! Come up and pull the cord working the knife, while we hold the condemned man down.'

The *sans-culotte* saw no way out of it, and mounted the steps. Sanson got the condemned man fastened to the plank, after a struggle; the assistant had to lie on top of him to keep him stretched out.

'Now, pull the cord!' Sanson ordered the youngster. But the latter was not so cocky now.

'I don't want to die!' cried Collot.

'Are you going to pull it, or aren't you?' growled Sanson.

The other went white as he did so. The knife flashed down, blood spurted, and the head dropped into the leather sack with a dull sound.

'You have to show it to the people,' said Sanson with a sneer. 'Unless you'd rather my assistant or I had that honour.'

'No, no,' retorted the patriot. And he slowly put his hand into the sack. Drawing out the bloody trophy by the hair, he held it in front of him but looked away. The crowd gave a great shout. Suddenly the amateur executioner dropped the head and fell to the boards. Charles-Henri laughed, then bent down and slapped the young man's face to bring him round. But this had no effect. Sanson felt his heart; the cruel *sans-culotte* was dead.

Some weeks later another drama ended in Charles-Henri losing his younger son. On August 27th, 1792, the Sansons were *louisoning* a man named Vimal and his accomplices, who had also been condemned for forging paper-money. The report of the executions in the *Moniteur* contained the statement: 'As the executioner picked up the head of one of the criminals to show it to the people, he fell from the scaffold and killed himself.'

So numerous were the Sansons that even journalists mistook one for another. This was not 'the executioner' who fell, but his younger son, Gabriel. He was killed outright, no doubt by fracturing his skull. His father and brother took the body back to the house in the rue Neuve-Saint-Jean, and Gabriel was buried in the family vault at St. Laurent's, bringing the total of coffins to ten.

The Paris Commune decided that the scaffold would remain in the Place du Carrousel for the execution of persons condemned for political crimes — which included the forging of paper-money, as that was prejudicial to the State credit. Other criminals, condemned for civil offences, were still executed in the Place de Grève. So that for a time the guillotine was moved backwards and forwards. Twenty-five heads fell in the Carrousel, thirty in front of the Hôtel de Ville. And Sanson had feared the new regime might suppress his office!

Meanwhile, the Paris mob had burst into the Tuileries, the Republic had been proclaimed, and Louis XVI and the royal family imprisoned in the Temple. The September massacres wiped out many aristocratic families. Nothing remained of the old regime.

Except one man — Charles-Henri Sanson. This was most extraordinary. The King had been deposed, the Parlements had been suppressed and the magistrates were in prison or had fled, feudal rights and taxes had been abolished, property of the Church and of aristocrats confiscated, legislation completely changed, the sale of offices and commissions had been ended — and yet the public executioner remained untouched. He and his forbears had whipped and executed the King's enemies during a century and more, yet Charles-Henri had come safely through the storm.

Nor were the bones of his ancestors molested. The tombs of French Kings were desecrated, but the Sanson vault in St. Laurent's was left alone. And, even after the 1765 decree forbidding burial within churches was confirmed by Republican laws, Charles-Henri was allowed to bury his sister, his uncle Gabriel and his aunt in the family vault, making thirteen in it. Nor were these burials conducted unobtrusively, but by day and in public, preceded by Mass celebrated by a priest who, however, had taken the constitutional oath.

No other similar exemption can be found during the period of revolutionary upheaval. Charles-Henri Sanson managed to make himself forgotten in the midst of all the troubles and disorders, while remaining a person much in the public view and despised and reviled by the Paris mob.

Confusion and disorder there were in plenty; and vagabonds and thieves made the most of it. 'Stop thief!' was a cry often heard. Then suddenly came news of a most audacious burglary — the Crown jewels had been stolen. These diamond bracelets, necklaces, and great gems, confiscated from Louis XVI and his family, had been placed in the Garde-meuble, the State furniture depository — in the building that is now the Navy Ministry, on the north side of the Place de la Concorde. Their total value had been estimated at 24 million *livres,* and all but half a million's worth had disappeared.

Eventually 17 persons including several women were arrested, accused of the theft or of receiving. The robbery had been a well-planned affair! Twelve death sentences were pronounced, though only five were carried out. The sentences specified that the executions were to take place 'in the Place de la Révolution, opposite the Garde-meuble,' the scene of the robbery.

So it was this theft of the Crown jewels that led to the guillotine being installed in the great square that used to be the Place Louis Quinze, and was later to have its name changed yet again to Place de la Concorde. And there, after its first five victims in October, 1792, it remained in place to execute so many more in the following months.

As Sanson, on that October day, let fall the slanting knife-edge that Louis XVI had sketched, he could never have imagined it would be used on that same King, in that same square, three months later!

CHAPTER SIX

The Sansons' climax: the death of Louis XVI

DURING THE evening of January 20th, 1793, the news spread that the Convention had rejected Louis XVI's request for a delay and had fixed his execution for the following morning.

Charles-Henri Sanson and his wife were about to celebrate the 28th anniversary of their wedding and also her 59th birthday. The servants had got out the best dinner-service and arranged flowers and fruit on the table. In previous years the Sansons had invited their friends to this double celebration, but the recent death of their younger son meant that on this occasion it was confined to the members of the household.

Newspapers in those days were unable to rush into print with a special edition. But any great news soon got round Paris, and Charles-Henri had already heard of the Assembly's decision. Without mentioning it to his wife, he went out to get confirmation. He intended going to the Palais de Justice, but first went round by the Tuileries gardens and to the Salle du Manège, where the Assembly was sitting. There, the ushers gave him the information he was seeking; no doubt remained that the climax of his sinister functions would be reached next morning. He turned back home, expecting his official instructions to have arrived during his absence or at least to be on their way.

On reaching the house he went straight to his study and saw the fatal warrant on his desk. There were some letters too, most of them anonymous. A few warned him that the King would be rescued during the journey from prison to the guillotine, and that if Sanson made any resistance he would be killed. Other letters implored him to assist the rescuers; or to delay proceedings on the scaffold, should the attack during the journey fail, to enable another to be made. And two or three letters just bluntly threatened him with death if he carried out the execution.

Charles-Henri then went to see if his wife had heard the news. Marie-Anne was a supporter of the monarchy and the church, and he felt that their anniversary dinner had better be postponed if she were already aware of what the morrow held. The matter was soon settled for him. He found Marie-Anne prostrate in an armchair, with their son bending over her and trying to bring her round. A young man, a stranger, was in the room; and it was he who had revealed the news of the execution to Marie-Anne by speaking of his plan to take the King's place on the scaffold.

This young fanatic proposed to dress himself up like the King, stuffing his waistcoat with rags to look as big and plump, and then to hide under the steps of the scaffold. When the King arrived, the executioner and the assistants would somehow smuggle him out of sight, and the young man would substitute himself.

Charles-Henri pointed out how mad the scheme was, and showed the young man out. There was no longer any question of having the celebration. The servants cleared the dining-table, and Charles-Henri, his wife and son, sat down instead to a simple supper by themselves. While they were eating in silence, a representative of the public-prosecutor was shown in. He had been sent to inform the public executioner that he was to go straight to the Place de la Révolution in the morning, instead of fetching the condemned man from prison, and wait for him on the scaffold. The excuse given for this change in traditional procedure was the conveyance to be used: Louis XVI would be taken to his execution in a closed carriage. Sanson had only an open cart.

Charles-Henri was not taken in by this explanation. He and his chief assistant could quite well travel in the carriage with the King. The real reason was that the authorities had got wind of plans to rescue the King; and, remembering the illicit printing-press discovered in Sanson's house, they had doubts about him. Two gendarmes were to accompany the King instead.

That night, Sanson lay down on his bed fully dressed. He kept listening for any strange noises, fearing an attack on his house, that an attempt might be made to steal or destroy the guillotine. His assistants had orders to leave with it at six in the morning, taking it in the cart to the Place de la Révolution.

At dawn, the drums of the National Guard began beating the assembly all over Paris. Each section had received orders to supply one battalion to line the route the King's carriage was to take. Henri Sanson — the son — was among those detailed from his section. He put on his uniform and picked up his gun. On the way out of the house he met his father dressed in a dark frock-coat and carrying a top-hat. Charles-Henri's drawn features and pale face were eloquent of his sleepless night. His two brothers, Charlemagne and Martin, were with him; they intended to accompany him, to help defend him if necessary, and had pistols and daggers concealed beneath their overcoats that were buttoned up to the neck because of the cold. Charles-Henri, too, had weapons on him.

Marie-Anne was there to see the four leave. She had spent part of the night in prayer, and for her the morning would be one of anguished waiting. In the street, Henri parted from his father and uncles and went towards St. Laurent's, the assembly-point for his battalion. By a coincidence, this unit was to stand guard round the scaffold. Henri was pleased to learn this, thinking he would be able to go to his father's assistance if he was attacked.

Charles-Henri and his brothers reached the Place de la Révolution at about eight-thirty, after pushing their way through the crowds gathering in the streets leading to the square. The scaffold and the guillotine had been erected, and Sanson's assistants in their leather aprons were having a snack. Charles-Henri, thinking the Royalists would succeed in rescuing the King, did not check over the machine that his assistants Le Gros and Barré had set up. 'It won't be needed,' he told himself.

At about that time, the carriage containing the King was setting out from the Temple. With him were his confessor, the *abbé* Edgeworth de Firmont — who had not taken the oath of allegiance to the State, but as he was of Irish nationality the authorities had closed their eyes to this — and the two gendarmes, a lieutenant named Lebrasse and a sergeant-major. Lebrasse was to be sent to the guillotine himself, fifteen months later.

Had these two gendarmes been instructed to kill the King if an attempt to rescue him seemed likely to succeed? So it was whispered at the time. The public-prosecutor knew he could not give such an order to Sanson who always maintained, 'Public executioners are not homicides.'

Hardly two dozen of the four or five hundred Royalists in the plot managed to reach their positions along the route, so great was the number of troops lining the streets and stopping anyone whose behaviour seemed suspicious. As the carriage and its escort were passing the Porte St. Denis four men with raised swords burst through the cordon shouting, 'Come on, Frenchmen! Help us save our King!'

But no one joined them, and in the ensuing confusion they managed to escape into the nearby streets, pursued by soldiers. Two got away — Baron de Batz and his secretary — but the other couple were cut down in the rue de Cléry.

The two gendarmes, though, had not killed the King. 'I don't know what their instructions were,' the abbé Edgeworth wrote later in his Memoirs, 'but unless they carried other weapons than those which were visible it would have been very difficult to kill the King; for only their muskets could be seen, and these were impossible to use in the carriage.'

News of the attempt swept along the waiting crowds and reached the Place de la Révolution long before the carriage with the King arrived there. But the story was of course distorted in the process; some versions gave the King as dead, others that he had escaped and got away. Charles-Henri and his brothers stood waiting on the scaffold, their gaze fixed on the point where the rue Royale joins the square, wondering whether or not they would see the cortège arrive. The scaffold had been placed more in the middle of the square, opposite the Hôtel de Crillon, so they were unable to look along the ci-devant rue Royale. Troops were drawn up in depth all round the scaffold, with drummers in the front ranks. A vast murmur was coming from the serried crowds behind, a sort of loud hum; but no cry or shout, no expressions of hate, joy, or pity. It was apparent that the waiting Parisians, whatever their political opinions, were aware of the exceptional gravity of the expected event.

Suddenly a great silence fell upon the colourfully-dressed multitude as the distant sound of trotting horses gradually became more distinct. The carriage and escort had increased their pace since the attack by the Porte St. Denis.

'Here they are,' murmured one of the three Sansons.

Many stories and legends grew up concerning the happenings on the scaffold and Sanson's attitude to the King. But a close eye-witness of the whole proceedings, the *abbé* Edgeworth, dispelled them all by giving the account in his Memoirs:

'As soon as the King stepped out of the carriage three execu-tioners surrounded him and made to take off his coat; but he pushed them disdainfully aside and took it off himself... The executioners, who had been taken aback for a moment by the proud bearing of the King, then seemed to recover their daring; they gathered round him again, wanting to tie his hands.

'What do you suppose you're going to do?' the King said, snatching his hands away.

'I must bind you,' replied one of the executioners.

'Bind me!' exclaimed the King indignantly. 'I will never consent to that!'

'The executioners insisted, raising their voices as though they would get help to do it forcibly.'

Louis XVI, fearing a violent scene, gazed at his confessor to ask for guidance. The priest murmured:

'Sire, I can only see in this fresh outrage a final similarity between Your Majesty and the God who is about to be his reward.'

'At these words the King raised his eyes to the heavens with an expression of grief impossible for me to describe. 'Certainly nothing less than His example is needed for me to submit to such an affront,' he said to me. Then, turning to the executioners he told them, 'Do what you will. I shall drink the cup to the dregs.' '

So they tied his hands behind his back, and Louis XVI mounted the steps of the scaffold helped only by the priest. At the top he 'slipped away, so to speak' from the arm of his confessor, and strode quickly across to the edge of the scaffold. 'With a single glance he imposed silence on the score or so of drummers just below him, and in a voice so loud that it must have been heard at the swing-bridge, he uttered these never-to-be-forgotten words:

'I die innocent of all the crimes imputed to me. I forgive the perpetrators of my death, and I pray God that the blood you are about to spill will never fall back on France.''

In maintaining that Louis XVI's voice 'must have been heard at the swing-bridge,' the good priest was exaggerating. This bridge was farther away than the present Pont de la Concorde, which succeeded it, being right at the corner of the square by the Tuileries gardens, nearly 400 yards from the scaffold; and there was a compact mass of people in between, who in the usual manner of Paris crowds were making lively comments on what was to them an incomprehensible discussion between Louis XVI and his executioners. Nor could many of them have heard Santerre, the military commander, interrupt the King's diatribe. Urging his horse forward, he cried, 'I've brought you here to die, not to harangue the crowd!' And to the executioners he ordered, 'Do your duty!'

The drums rolled, Louis XVI surrendered himself to his fate. At 10.22 Sanson's assistant, Le Gros, held up the dripping head for the crowd to see. And they greeted it with shouts of 'Vive la Nation! Vive la République!'

Sanson's cart carried away the King's decapitated body, which was placed in a long wicker-basket. It was buried in the Madeleine cemetery, Sanson's assistants first transferring it to a coffin of pinewood and then covering that with quicklime.

After leaving the cemetery, Sanson's horse shied at something and the cart overturned. The wicker-basket was thrown to the ground and burst open, spattering clots of blood. A number of passers-by hurried to gather drops of the martyred King's blood, wiping round the inside of the basket with a handkerchief, a cravat, or a piece of plain paper. One person was even seen to take a couple of dice from his pocket and rub them in the crimson deposit.

During the next few days, rumours went round that Sanson had taken money for allowing this to be done. One newspaper, *Le Thermomètre du Jour*, went further; and was obliged to print the following in its issue of January 29th:

'The buttons from Louis Capet's jacket, bits of his shirt and locks of his hair have been sold at high prices. The executioner Sanson, accused of having had a hand in this new kind of trade, has written to clear himself in these terms: 'I learn it is being said that I am selling the hair of Louis Capet. If any has been sold, such squalid dealings can only be the work of knaves. The truth is that I have not allowed any of my personnel to take or carry off the slightest amount.' '

The words 'I have not allowed' show that Charles-Henri had at least to take steps to prevent it. Possibly his assistants or one of his brothers wanted to go in for these profitable dealings. But he was still too much of a believer to permit an insult to the dead, and royalist enough to have no part in trading in relics of the King.

Did he have a Mass said for the martyred monarch? — as Balzac later wrote. This is impossible to confirm, but several circumstances show that it may well have taken place. Although Balzac used his fertile imagination to describe the episode, he obtained the gist of some of it from Henri Sanson when the latter was an old man. The story began with Jean-Baptiste Sanson's healing of Chesneau, the armourer of the Comte de Charolais. Chesneau had remained on friendly terms with the Sanson family. In 1793, although he supported the ideals of the Revolution he was still in contact with his old employer and family. Among them was a nun who had gone into hiding with a priest and another nun; all three were living in an attic in the Faubourg St. Martin, and Chesneau used to take them what money and food he could.

Charles-Henri Sanson knew, through Chesneau, of their existence and where they were living. On the evening of January

21st, so Balzac's account goes, Charles-Henri went to see them. The two old nuns were scared at the sight of this unknown intruder, thinking it was someone come to arrest them at last; but the priest — one who had refused to take the oath to the State — received him more calmly. The priest had been told by Chesneau of the sentence pronounced on the King, but had said nothing to his two companions in hiding. When the guns had boomed out that morning, announcing 'the death of the tyrant', the priest had refrained from saying how the sound had sent a chill through his heart.

The two nuns were therefore greatly surprised to hear the visitor ask for a Mass to be said 'for the repose of an illustrious soul'. The priest less so; he realised to whom it referred. The nuns helped him prepare an altar; the first intimation they had of the King's death was on hearing the priest make an addition to the liturgy: '*Et remitte scetus regicidis sicut Ludovicus eis remisit semet ipse.*' (And forgive the regicides as Louis XVI has forgiven them.)

No Mass could have had less pomp — wrote Balzac — than this one celebrated on an old, worm-eaten chest-of-drawers, in an attic where icy draughts came through cracks in the walls; yet none could have been more solemn. When it was over, the priest asked the name of his visitor. Charles-Henri declined to give it, but as he was leaving he drew a small cardboard box from his pocket. 'This will gratify you far more than a modest offering,' he said as he handed it to the priest.

It contained the handkerchief used by Louis XVI on his last journey. The fine cambric still smelt of the King, and there were tiny rust-like marks on it. The King had been holding it, clenched in his tied hands, when the knife fell.

CHAPTER SEVEN

Charles-Henri, Keystone of the Terror

ACCORDING TO Michaud's massive *Biographie Universelle*, Charles-Henri Sanson died in 1793, six months after executing Louis XVI. 'So it was not he,' says the article in question, 'who executed Marie-Antoinette, Malesherbes, Danton, Robespierre, and so many others.' Later, the Larousse Dictionary also gave Charles-Henri's death as 1793 — and still does. Many historians and biographers have taken these entries as a fact. But the truth is that Charles-Henri lived on until 1806. He left it to his son Henri to guillotine the Queen; nearly all the other victims of the Terror, though, were executed by Charles-Henri or under his supervision.

There exist at least four documents — all in the Archives Nationales — which prove this:

In Floréal of Year 11 (April, 1794) Charles-Henri wrote to the Minister of Justice complaining about his financial situation; his expenses had increased enormously, and he was unable to make ends meet.

On the 13th of Fructidor, Year 111 (August 30th, 1795) he sent in his resignation. Referring to himself in the third person, the public executioner wrote: 'He has carried out the functions of his office for 43 years. He suffers from kidney trouble and is unable to continue his duties. He applies for an annual assistance of 1,000 *livres*, which executioners without employment who have spent long years in the service enjoy; he is quite prepared to take up his functions again as soon as his health permits.'[1]

---

[1] There are no spelling mistakes in the French of this letter (as in a previous one of Charles-Henri's quoted). He was no doubt helped with the writing of it.

To judge by this letter, then, Charles-Henri gave up his office to his son in 1795, when the Terror was over.

Charles-Henri made a fresh request for a pension in January, 1802. It is referred to in a letter from the liquidator of the Public Debt, dated the 4th of Pluviôse, Year X.

The pension was no doubt refused; as Charles-Henri, in spite of his age and although 'suffering from an infirmity' (says the above-mentioned letter), took up the functions of executioner again. To inaugurate his reappearance on the scaffold he was given a murderess to guillotine. The day after, May 6th, 1802, he addressed a petition — the fourth proof that he lived beyond 1793 — to the First Consul. He referred to the violent scenes that took place whenever a woman was guillotined, and asked Bonaparte to reprieve all women condemned to death.

And, finally, there is the date on the tombstone in Montmartre cemetery — died July 4th, 1806.

So no possible doubt remains; Charles-Henri, the great Sanson, did not breathe his last during the Terror.

Nevertheless, during that terrible period he directed executions much more often than he actually performed them. There were occasions when he did not even appear on the scaffold. There was no one permanent public executioner. Sometimes Henri supervised the assistants for his father, sometimes it was one of the uncles, Charlemagne or Martin. A Sanson was always there, but not the same one. Only the two chief assistants, Le Gros and Barré, went on guillotining without faltering. It was Le Gros, that coarse brute, who slapped the guillotined head of Charlotte Corday.

But for the Parisians, unaware of any of this, there was only one Sanson. And naturally it was the most flamboyant, the most cruel of the four, and the youngest too.

This explains why Larivière, one of Marie-Antoinette's jailers, said that 'Sanson, then a young man,' had cut off the Queen's hair. But in 1793 Charles-Henri was 55.

It explains, too, why Mrs. Elliot, an Englishwoman who had been the mistress of the Duc d'Orléans and who was imprisoned for several months during the French Revolution, wrote in her

Memoirs that the turnkey took her to have a drink with 'an elegant, handsome young man' whose name was Sanson. This handsome young man did not treat his future clients with any regard. When Mrs. Elliot learnt his name, the turnkey — who was having a glass with them — said to her: 'You ought to make friends with this citizen; he might be called on to decapitate you.'

'I almost fainted,' recounted the young woman, 'especially when the executioner put his hand round my neck and said, 'It would soon be over, your neck is so long and slender! If I have to despatch you, you won't even notice it.''

Henri felt much less repulsion than his father, then, for their odious tasks. He was pitiless and indifferent to the victims' anguish, and shrugged his shoulders at their entreaties.

Charles-Henri, though, was capable of gentleness and compassion. When taking Charlotte Corday to her execution in his cart, he watched her more like a father than an executioner. Seeing that she was being jolted about, he advised her to lean against the side. 'It's a long way, isn't it?' he murmured. She gave him a sad little smile. 'But we're sure to get there!' she said.

Just as the cart reached the square, Sanson stepped in front of her. Charlotte Corday realised it was to hide the sight of the guillotine from her, but she leant forward and said, 'I've a right to be curious; I've never seen it before.'

Another instance of the humanity of the master-executioner can be found in the visit he made to Camille Desmoulins' father-in-law.

Desmoulins, who was guillotined with Danton on April 5th, 1794, had handed a small oval locket to Sanson. It contained a curl of his wife's hair — Lucile Desmoulins had been arrested the previous day. Desmoulins, fearful of the precious souvenir falling into profane hands, had asked Sanson to promise to take it to Lucile's father, citizen Duplessis.

Charles-Henri bore a grudge against Desmoulins for writing: 'I call a spade a spade, and Sanson a common hangman.' But he had agreed to carry out the pamphleteer's last wish, and went to the house in the rue du Théâtre-Français where Desmoulins had lived, not knowing his father-in-law's address. The concierge gave it to Sanson — rue des Arcs, formerly rue Saint André-des-Arts. When he got there Charles-Henri handed the locket to a servant. 'I happened to be present when Camille was executed,' he said, 'and he asked me to give this to his wife's parents.' Charles-Henri disliked the idea of meeting them, and at once left without giving his name.

He had hardly gone a hundred yards when he heard someone running after him. Turning round, he saw it was the servant; she was followed by Monsieur Duplessis. The latter asked Sanson back to his rooms, to tell him about the execution of his son-in-law. Charles-Henri refused at first; but while they stood there talking he feared that some passer-by might recognise him and denounce him to Lucile's father, and so horrify the poor man. He therefore agreed to go back with Duplessis.

The two had just sat down in a well-furnished room when a child started to cry in the apartment. Duplessis went out, and returned with a little boy who looked ill. 'He's their son,' he said to Sanson.

Then, referring to Camille Desmoulins without naming him, he asked, 'You were there? You saw him?'

Sanson nodded.

Dreading to utter the word 'death', the other said, 'Like a man of spirit, as a Republican, didn't he?'

Charles-Henri, avoiding a reply which would have been disagreeable to the royalist ideas he still held, declared, 'His last words were for those he loved.'

'And her?' groaned Duplessis. 'My daughter, poor Lucile. Will they be as pitiless towards her? To think I shan't be able to be with her at the end ... that to send me her last farewell she'll have nobody but the wretched hangman!'

These words sent a shudder through Charles-Henri. He saw Duplessis, who was walking up and down the room, stop by the mantelpiece, knock over a bust representing Liberty and send it smashing to the ground. Charles-Henri felt dismayed and wished he had never given in to the unhappy man's insistence.

A woman of 50 or so came into the room; she carried her

years with distinction, but her fine face was ravaged by anguish. The cloak she was wearing showed she had come from the street. She stumbled across and fell into Duplessis's arms. 'She's doomed — she has to appear before the tribunal the day after tomorrow!'

It was Lucile's mother.

Charles-Henri, telling the story of this meeting when he was an old man, said: 'I was terrified at the thought of being recognised by this woman whose daughter's happiness I had destroyed, and whose daughter herself I should very likely have to destroy too. I fled from the house as though I had committed a crime.'

Three days after that meeting he had to guillotine Lucile Desmoulins. She was 23, and went to her death smiling and gracious, adorned as though for a ball. There was nothing studied or affected in this display of courage; just the joy of going to join her husband, her love.

Charles-Henri wrapped her hair, which had been cut off at the Conciergerie, in a sheet of paper and gave the packet to one of the young Savoyards who were acting as messengers, to take to the Duplessis couple. The youngster knew Sanson by sight, but not his name nor who he was. The executioner thus denied himself, by refraining from adding to the tribulations of the unfortunate parents, the vain satisfaction of showing that a man such as he had a heart.

The citizens Sanson and their aides had more work to do than ever, after the setting up of the *Tribunal Révolutionnaire*. Its members, nominated by the Convention, were given the task of pronouncing verdicts — against which no appeal was possible — on conspirators and counter-revolutionaries.

There were plenty of one and the other to be found in every class of society. The Tribunal sent the Sansons noblemen and footmen, bishops and sextons, generals and privates, respectable housewives and prositutes, the old and the young, the intelligent and the imbecile.

Among their judges were genuine titled people; one of the most implacable was the *ci-devant* Marquis d'Antonelle. Another, the Marquis de Monflabert, concealed his title under the pseudonym

of Leroy. Then, finding this had a royalist flavour, he changed it
for the patriotic nickname of *Dix Août* (the day the Monarchy
was overthrown).

The Tribunal was composed of a record number of members
— a president and a vice-president, 17 judges and 5 deputy-
judges, 60 jurymen, and a public-prosecutor — who sent the
guillotine its daily ration of victims. Between the date of the
setting-up of the *Tribunal Révolutionnaire* (March 11th, 1793)
and the end of the Terror (July 17th, 1794) the Sansons and
their assistants let the knife fall 1,256 times — errors and
omissions excepted — in the Place de la Révolution; and 1,376
times in the Place de la Bastille or in the Place du Trône-
Renversé, where they moved the guillotine to on June 9th, 1794.
In all, the Sansons 'despatched' 2,632 people in 502 days — an
average of 5.24.[1]

Few of these executions have not some anecdote, some
courageous action or grisly happening attached to them.

When Marie-Anne Sanson heard of the verdict on the Queen
she said to her husband: 'Condemned to death — her too! All
this blood spilt will fall on our heads. Charles, by serving the
interests and passions of a party, you are becoming an accomplice
to its crimes. If you knew what I went through the day ... of the
King. Don't carry out this other murder.'

Charles-Henri gave way to his wife's pleas. His place was
taken by his son — which amounted to the same thing for
Marie-Anne. So it was to Henri Sanson, and not to Charles-
Henri, that the Queen spoke her last words, after accidentally
treading on his foot: 'Pardon, Monsieur.'

Madame Roland, whose famous salon had been frequented by
the Girondins, was sent to the guillotine at the same time as a

---

[1] About 20,000 are estimated to have been guillotined in the provinces by other
executioners. Although the crimes of one period are no excuse for those of another,
the above figures seem small when compared with the six million Jews and two
million other people exterminated in the Nazi concentration camps. In three years,
that gives an average of 7,300 murders a day. From the guillotine to the gas-
chamber, great progress had been made!

The French Revolution had at least the excuse of upholding the Declaration of
the Rights of Man. Whereas the Nazis trampled on it.

man named Lamarche, and they made the journey in the cart together. The order in which executions were to be carried out had been determined by the public-prosecutor, Fouquier-Tinville, since the death of the Girondins; and he had put Madame Roland's name first. But when the cart reached the scaffold she saw Lamarche begin to tremble. 'I'd like to spare you the horror of seeing my blood flow,' she said to him. 'You go first.'

Lamarche was about to, but Sanson objected that the order could not be changed.

'Surely you haven't been ordered to refuse a lady's last wish,' retorted Madame Roland with a forced smile.

Charles-Henri gave way, and his assistants took the half-fainting Lamarche up to the guillotine. Madame Roland saw his head fall, and then climbed the steps to the scaffold by herself.

The execution of Madame du Barry was a different matter. When Charles-Henri went to 'take delivery' of her at the Conciergerie he remembered that he had known her in his youth, long before she slipped into the royal bed. He now found a woman in her fifties, still beautiful but plump, and with her face made haggard by fear and anguish. Three of Sanson's assistants had to struggle with her in order to cut off her hair and tie her hands. Charles-Henri turned his head, not trusting himself to intervene.

In the cart, on the way to the guillotine, the hapless woman gave shrieks of despair that astonished the crowds gathered along the route. Most of the condemned went to their deaths with resignation, some with a smile on their lips ... they knew what they were dying for — the Monarchy or the Church, or the Republic and Liberty. Jeanne Gomard du Barry did not know. For having slid naked into bed with a King? Was that sufficient reason?

'Good citizens, I'm innocent!' she cried to the crowds jeering at her. 'I'm one of the people, like you. Don't let me die!'

She would have fallen several times, jolted about in the cart, if Henri Sanson had not held her. He had gone along too, well aware that his father — who had perhaps confided in him — would not be up to directing her execution. And in fact she did turn towards the man who had admired her in her young days.

'No,' she pleaded, her arms tied, her breast half-uncovered by her earlier struggles, 'no, you won't kill me, will you?'

When the cart reached the Place de la Révolution the assistants had to struggle with her again to get her up to the scaffold.

The following day, Charles-Henri had to guillotine an ex-member of the Assembly named Noel, who had been proscribed. In the cart, the condemned man asked Sanson if it was true, as rumours reaching the Conciergerie made out, that Madame du Barry had been so lacking in courage. And when Sanson replied in the affirmative, the other exclaimed: 'I hope your men have given the knife a good wipe! The blood of a prostitute ought not to soil the neck of a republican!'

A little while later came the turn of Baron de Dietrich, who had been mayor of Strasbourg. It was he who had suggested to Rouget de Lisle to compose a 'Hymn to the Army of the Rhine' — which later became the *Marseillaise*. As Le Gros was strapping him to the plank, Dietrich said to the executioner: 'You've already guillotined some good republicans, but none as devoted as I to the nation.'

Another no less convinced republican was General de Gontaut-Biron, Duc de Lauzun. He had won battles in Germany and then in the Vendée, but nevertheless had been accused and sentenced to death. When Charles-Henri went to collect him at the Conciergerie he found the General sitting at table in the turnkey's room with a plate of oysters and a bottle of white wine before him; he was gathering strength to face his last adversary.

'You won't mind giving me time to have another dozen, will you?' he said to Sanson.

Then, after a short silence, he added: 'Sanson, you need to be in form, in your job. Sit yourself down, and eat and drink with me! Citizen turnkey, let's have some more oysters!'

The executioner and his victim drank to the health of the nation; and the jailer was given a glass, too. Then General de Biron's hair was cut off and his hands tied behind his back. Going along in the cart, he sang army ditties. A soldier who had served under him called, '*Adieu, mon général!*' To which he replied, '*Au revoir, mon camarade!*'

Nobody dared to lay a hand on the soldier, nor abuse the General. Noticing this, and other indications, Charles-Henri wrote in the Diary he kept spasmodically: 'Since the death of Madame du Barry the people have become less set against the condemned. If they all shouted and struggled as she did, the guillotine wouldn't last much longer.'

The name of Adrien Lamourette, the Bishop of Lyon, had become known to Parisians because of an eloquent appeal for union that he had made in the Assembly in July, 1792, being then a member of that body; so eloquent was it that at the end the members had embraced each other with cries of joy and expressions of forgiveness. And this scene of general reconciliation — forgotten next day — was popularly called 'The Lamourette Kiss'. This was remembered by the crowds when Lamourette was being taken to the guillotine, and he was taunted by jeering cries of 'Kiss Charlie, then, Lamourette!'

Undaunted by it all, the Bishop turned to Charles-Henri and said: 'Just before my end I shall embrace all humanity through you. However crazy and furious it becomes, it's still humanity.'

He kept his promise, kissing Charles-Henri on the cheek as he was about to be placed under the knife. The victim kissing the executioner — no other period could have produced such a scene, to be engraved!

Nor such a sight as the magistrates of the Old Régime (whose sentences Charles-Henri had carried out for the past 40 years) going to their deaths with the proud serenity of heroes of the classical age. There were 31 of them condemned by the Tribunal, and they walked to the three waiting tumbrils in order of precedence, grave and dignified, as though it were a procession to open the old Parlement.

Charles-Henri was dumbfounded. 'I won't be able to,' he stammered to the President of the Upper Court, Bochart de Sarron. 'Not you, Monsieur le Président!'

'Do what the law requires,' the condemned man retorted. 'Even though unjust, the law is still the law.'

Another occasion when Charles-Henri felt his nerve failing

was the carrying out of sentences on 'The Virgins of Verdun'. These girls had gone dressed in white to present flowers to the commander of the Prussian army, the Duke of Brunswick, when he entered Verdun at the head of his victorious troops. Three weeks later the French won the battle of Valmy and drove the enemy back towards the frontier. The girls were denounced and, with their parents, taken to Paris. The Tribunal refused to take into consideration the youth of many of them, and 32 death sentences were pronounced and carried out. An exception was made for the remaining two, Barbe Henry and Claire Tabouillot, because they had only been 16 at the time of their *crime*. They were sentenced to twenty years' imprisonment and to stand for six hours on the scaffold where their friends and relatives had been guillotined the previous day.

Charles-Henri went to fetch the two girls. Although mourning their relatives, they had dressed in white as when greeting the Prussian commander. On the scaffold, each girl was attached to one of the uprights of the guillotine, and a placard was hung round her neck. The words on it were: 'A traitor to the country, I helped deliver Verdun to the enemy by supplying him with food, money, and munitions.'

The scaffold stank with dried blood. It was difficult to clean below it, because a metal net had been put round to prevent dogs licking the blood that trickled down. The executioner and his assistants were used to the horrible stench, and the victims of the guillotine were not there long enough to be affected by it; but Claire Tabouillot and Barbe Henry soon began to feel sick, especially as some of the recent blood was that of their own relatives. At the end of an hour the Henry girl fainted away. Charles-Henri untied her, to help bring her round; there was only the plank of the guillotine for her to sit on. Then the other girl went white and her eyes started to roll.

Someone in the crowd found the courage to shout, 'That's enough!' A few others joined in, timidly at first.

Charles-Henri told his son to borrow a horse from one of the gendarmes and hurry to the Palais de Justice and ask permission to end the girls' punishment. Henri found Naudin, Fouquier-

Tinville's deputy, and he agreed to give the necessary orders, sending some constables to take the two girls off to prison.

A revolution is like a volcano in eruption; and the worst of the eruption during the French Revolution was the Terror. Whether it was necessary, to destroy those opposed to the widespread social changes under way, can be argued endlessly. But pure patriots such as Robespierre, Couthon, Saint-Just, and even Carnot believed it was. And Charles-Henri Sanson was its instrument: he was the Keystone of the Terror.

He could not argue against the sentences he was ordered to put into effect. But, being still a royalist at heart, he preferred to guillotine republicans rather than monarchists. When the *Tribunal Révolutionnaire* sent him a Schneider or a Jourdan the Head-chopper he performed his task with satisfaction. Both of these men, moreover, were cruel and heartless monsters.

Euloge Schneider, a defrocked priest, had become public-prosecutor at Strasbourg and used the Terror to his own profit. His *Tribunal Révolutionnaire* was a mobile one. He, with his judges and jurymen, clerk, executioner and guillotine, travelled from town to town all over Alsace, escorted by hussars who had a death's head painted on their scabbards. He set up his court of justice in a town-hall, a barn, or even under an oak-tree — in imitation of St. Louis. By raising taxes to pay his cavalcade, by giving orders and judgments and not having them recorded, and sentencing parents who refused him their daughter for a night, Schneider made himself hated by the whole population.

But Saint-Just was waiting for him in Strasbourg, and had him arrested. He was sent to Paris, condemned to death, and handed over to Sanson. He was still conceited enough to try to show off, and told Sanson his neck was so thick that the knife would be blunted by contact with it.

'That'll make it all the more painful for you, then,' Sanson retorted, 'and will be your punishment.'

At these words, the rogue burst into tears. He sobbed all the way in the cart, and when strapped to the plank stuttered 'Monsieur, monsieur, monsieur . . .' and got no further.

Jourdan the Head-chopper had kept a tavern in Paris in 1789; he claimed it was he, and not Desnot the cook, who had had the *honour* of cutting off the head of Monsieur de Launay, the governor of the Bastille, with a butcher's knife. Later, when the Paris mob invaded the château of Versailles, Jourdan chopped off the heads of three of the Household Guard. Instead of being congratulated for these crimes, as he expected, he had to flee to escape arrest, and got to the Papal city of Avignon, which did not then belong to the French State. By 1791 he was at the head of a band of brigands who were terrorising the countryside under the pretext of annexing the district to France. Some while later, having got his name included in a general amnesty, he was put in command of the gendarmes in two Provençal *départements*. He then used this authority to his own ends by having people arrested and threatening to send them before the tribunal if they did not pay him for their release. Like Schneider, he took any girl he fancied unless her parents paid his price for not molesting her.

But justice finally caught up with him. The Committee of Public Safety in Paris had him arrested, and in May, 1794, he was carted off to the guillotine. He had bought several bottles from the concierge of the prison, to give himself courage; and was half-drunk when the scaffold was reached. 'Here — sleep with your mistress!' jeered Charles-Henri, pushing him under the knife.

Although the Republic was in full swing, many men — Robespierre for one — kept to the habit of wearing a powdered wig, as in the days of 'the tyrant'. But Charles-Henri and his son could not afford to do so; one splash of blood, and a white wig was spoilt. Charles-Henri still wore his tall hat crammed on his mop of sandy hair; and every morning, draped in his long black frock-coat, went to the Palais de Justice where the Tribunal was preparing the daily batch of heads.

The numbers kept increasing, and Charles-Henri was obliged to recruit more assistants. In the two years from 1792 to 1794 they gradually went from four to nine. At one moment he almost took on an Englishman, only refusing him because he said he wanted the experience for a short time, just long enough to get used to strong emotions. The execution staff thus amounted to thirteen, with Charles-Henri, his two brothers and his son. There were also the carpenter and his workmen, though they did not come under the Sansons.

Charles-Henri had two carts for taking the condemned from prison to the guillotine; when the number on any one day was too great, he hired additional tumbrils. Seven extra were necessary on a morning in June, 1794. The Tribunal sent him 54 people in one batch, all sentenced to death for a 'plot' against the Republic. Fouquier-Tinville had the knack of trumping up charges on such a grand scale; he made accomplices and fellow-plotters out of people who had never known each other before appearing in court together. In this case, noblemen and servants and house-wives found themselves linked; among these innocents and half-guilty, these royalists, republicans, fanatics, and simple-minded, were an actress and her 18-year-old maid, Nicole Bouchard, who *did not look more than 14.*

The nine tumbrils drew out from the Palais de Justice carrying the 54 victims dressed in the red cloaks of parricides — for had they not made an attempt on the lives of Robespierre and Collot-d'Herbois, fathers of the people? The procession rumbled slowly round Paris for three hours, the wheels jolting over the rough cobbles and sending the prisoners lurching against each other time and again. Police agents went through the streets, stirring up the people and shouting, 'Here comes the red Mass! Death to Robespierre's attackers!'

But for the first time murmurs were heard of 'So many victims for one man?'

There were some women in the first cart, and as they were young and pretty they drew exclamations of pity from the crowds along the way. When Nicole Bouchard was seen in the next cart, the people's mood changed to indignation. 'No children!' was a cry heard in a dozen different places.

Charles-Henri was in the leading cart; he hardly dared look back at the frail, delicate young girl who, with the selflessness of the heroines of her day, was trying to console her weeping mistress.

In the Place du Trône, the butchery began; every two minutes a head fell. Young Nicole was the ninth to mount the scaffold, held by two of Sanson's assistants. As she was taken past him, the public executioner raised his tall hat and bowed with respect. 'Citizens,' she murmured as she was being strapped to the plank, 'am I all right like this?'

Charles-Henri turned his head away. A mist came over his eyes, and he began to feel giddy. His brother Martin worked the guillotine, and then said to him, 'Go back home, you're not well; I'll manage alone.'

Charles-Henri went down the steps without a word and walked slowly away, heavy-eyed and with aching limbs. At table that evening he asserted to his wife that he could see bloodstains on the white cloth.

At that period, mid-1794, Henri was no longer assisting his father. Not because the Sanson functions disgusted him — his hardness was a natural armour against their effect — but because his country needed fighting men to thrust back the invading armies. Most of the troops had gone to war, and replacements were required at home where trouble was brewing.

Henri was a powerfully-built man of 27 whose height added to his presence; Mrs. Elliot had described him as 'an elegant and handsome young man'. He was beginning to lose his hair, which made his forehead look unnaturally high. He never raised his voice, but his toneless expression gave firmness to his words. This calm air of authority had caused him to be nominated, in 1792, to the rank of sergeant in the National Guard.

One Sunday in October, 1793 — a few days after he had guillotined the Queen — Henri heard drums beating the assembly and hurried out to St. Laurent's, the meeting-place of his section and which had been turned into a secular Temple of Reason. There he learnt that the section was required to form an artillery company; and afterwards, as usually happened then, to elect its captain.

Henri, to his great surprise, was elected. As he knew nothing whatever about artillery, he wanted to refuse this honour.

'What does that matter?' exclaimed one of the others. 'We've got a good instructor; in a month, you'll know all there is to know.'

So Henri became captain of the newly-formed 48th company of the Paris Artillery Corps. He had command of two guns and 50 men, and his pay was 7 *livres* and 10 *sols* for each day the company was on manœuvres or fighting; the rest of the time he got nothing and could do as he wished. At first, he had only to get into uniform once or twice a week, and when not training with his company he assisted his father as executioner.

But suddenly he found himself obliged to give all his time to military duties. He was transferred to the gendarmerie — the reason is not known — and was appointed captain of the 2nd Company, which came under the orders of Lieutenant-Colonel Botot-Dumesnil; this officer commanded the force of gendarmes responsible for keeping law and order at the Conciergerie and the Palais de Justice, and in the streets where the tumbrils passed on their way to the guillotine. So instead of standing in one of them as executioner, Captain Sanson found himself escorting them in his blue uniform with yellow facings and wearing a two-cornered hat with a red pompon.

He moved from home and rented what would today be called a *garconnière*, a bachelor-flat, near the Châtelet, at No. 37 in the rue Saint Jacques-la-Boucherie. In the spring of 1794 came another change. He was posted back to the artillery, and ordered to go with 150 soldiers and 6 guns to Coulommiers, in the Brie country, some 40 miles east of Paris; the peasants there had risen in revolt. But on arrival with his small force, Henri found that a squadron of cavalry had already put down the local uprising.

The authorities, fearing a fresh outbreak, ordered Henri to remain in Coulommiers with his men. For some weeks he lived in the cavalry officers' mess, enjoying the unusual experience of being treated as a fellow comrade. He was recalled to Paris at a time when the Terror was showing signs of abating. Under his orders were now 25 artillerymen and their two guns, and a lieutenant with 30 foot-soldiers; for the next month or so Henri did little more than inspect his soldiers from time to time at the police-posts they were guarding, and take his gunners to fire some practice-rounds.

His father was more than ever weary of it all; he only continued in office in order to save himself from becoming a victim of the Terror. Indispensable as he was, Charles-Henri was not afraid to put on paper what less prudent people would not have dared say under cover, during this period when the slightest indiscretion led to the guillotine. One day he sent the Minister for Justice his 'Observations on the existence of the Paris executioner'. This long and tedious piece of writing is worth a résumé, for it was both a complaint and a criticism.

As a result of the *livre* being replaced by the franc, a decree dated June 13th, 1793, had converted Charles-Henri's yearly salary of 17,000 *livres* into 10,000 francs. By the same decree he received an additional 1,000 francs for each assistant, to a total of four; and his pay was increased by 3,000 francs while the government remained a *revolutionary* one. This gave him an annual income of 17,000 francs.

What were his expenses in 1794? He paid his four chief assistants 1,800 francs a year, which was the salary they demanded; and 800 francs to each of the three extra assistants. The house where he lodged them cost him 3,000 a year in rent. So for his assistants alone he paid out 12,600 — and received 4,000 for them.

The upkeep of his two carts and the fodder for the horses he reckoned to be 40 francs a day. When he had to hire other carts, each one cost 15 francs a day and he gave 5 francs to the driver. He also had to supply the placards when malefactors were put in the pillory, and he estimated the cost at 1,500 francs a year. Then there were the wicker-baskets for carrying away the corpses; the straw and the sawdust, nails, grease for the grooves of the guillotine, straps for the plank (they got worn through at an alarming rate), burial expenses and tips to the grave-diggers — all of which had to be paid from Sanson's pocket.

He concluded his letter — referring to himself in the third person, as he usually did on paper — as follows:

. 'He cannot expend 30 to 35,000 francs a year with the 10,000 he draws... He asks for the closest enquiries to be made, and after that has been done, for, *primo*, him to be repaid; *next*, if these functions can be carried out at lower cost, for another person to be so charged, as he cannot manage to carry on, as he will have to give it all up if he is not repaid and does not obtain justice.'

Nobody else in France, in 1794, could have employed language such as that. The nation had all Europe against it. 'Victory or death' was not just a patriotic formula; any general who lost a battle, any civil servant who jibbed at his orders, was sent to the guillotine. The whole country, to back up the army, had to submit to a national discipline. By protesting against his salary, demanding repayment and threatening to 'give it all up,' any servant of the State other than Sanson would have been declared a traitor and put in prison; a brief appearance on the scaffold would have been the only result of such a letter.

For merely having said of Robespierre, 'I wanted to see what a tyrant is like,' young Cécile Renault had been guillotined. The same had happened to a housewife who grumbled about the high cost of meat, and to a blacksmith who stopped work before the forge closed down for the day. For saying 'France is too big for a republic,' a veteran soldier had been handed over to the public executioner.

And here was the executioner himself daring to complain! He must have been sure of his ground... Charles-Henri Sanson, the head of the large family of executioners at work in Paris and the provinces, was in fact indispensable to the regime and he knew it. Even the members of the Assembly had become little more than stooges, many of them in constant fear of their lives. Through patriotism or dread of the consequences, everyone kept quiet. But Sanson did more than raise his voice; he put pen to paper. Although he knew there was talk of him being a royalist, he laid himself open to attack. Under the screen of his expenses-account, he showed his all-powerful, terrible superiors how weary of it all he was. He did not fear being told 'It's worth ruining oneself in the country's service.' If he had not been the public executioner, he would have been executed. He guillotined many unfortunate people who had dared to do or say much less than he had done.

But his complaints were examined by the authorities, his accounts gone into item by item. A long report was made, and a copy sent to him. The conclusion was, nevertheless, that his salary and allowances ought to be sufficient for him, and that any further application on his part would be rejected.

The only way left to Charles-Henri to make ends meet was to find some racket that would bring in the money. There were plenty of flourishing rackets just then — what would in our day be called black markets, in leather, sugar, paper, soap, and saltpetre for the making of gunpowder. A curious thing was that these operators scorned the growing danger of being brought before the *Tribunal Révolutionnaire*. They would never have risked making imprudent remarks; but cornering stocks of essential food and commodities, cheating and robbing their fellow-beings, seemed to them less dangerous.

What were the goods that Charles-Henri made money from? It is difficult to describe this racket without feelings of great disgust. The public executioner had already been accused, earlier in the century, of selling *fat from the hanged*, 'excellent for rheumatic pains'. A journalist of the times, Sébastien Mercier, wrote that the executioner sold it quite openly; and that he also sold corpses to surgeons, and kept others for his own attempts at dissection. Sanson had no time for any of that during the Terror. Instead, he began to hire out heads — the severed heads of people he had guillotined! To one person only, but one who prospered from this shameful business.

Admittedly, that is only a popular rumour of the times; but most rumours have an element of truth in them. In any case, the opportunity certainly existed; the facts of this astounding and macabre story are as follows:

A Swiss from Berne by the name of Christophe Curtius, who

made wax-models of human organs and sold them to anatomists and medical schools, moved to Strasbourg in 1760. While on a visit to Paris he showed examples of his work to the Prince de Conti, who was so struck by the novelty that he pressed Curtius to set up his workroom in Paris and open a Waxwork Show, which would be something entirely new for the times. Curtius came to Paris with his niece, Marie Grosholtz, and eventually opened a gallery in the rue St. Honoré. He modelled busts of well-known people in wax, from paintings or sketches of them, and put the results on show. People began to go and sit to him; his studio became a meeting-place for artists and writers and society ladies, while Marie Grosholtz acted as hostess and served tea to them. The public paid to go into the gallery and see the waxwork busts of celebrities of the period.

Encouraged by this success, Curtius began to make full-length models and groups, and dressed them up. He thus put on show, for instance, Louis XVI welcoming the envoys of the Nawab of Mysore, and foreign princesses having tea with the children of the Royal family. Curtius soon had enough money to open another Waxwork Show. This was in the Boulevard du Temple and was called 'The Robbers' Cave'. It showed cut-throats at their work, and in the last room were notorious brigands being tortured after capture or having justice meted out to them in the form of the wheel, the gallows, or the block — to give the public plenty of sensationalism, and perhaps to point a moral.

Curtius had obtained the details for these set-pieces from specialists in the subject, including of course Charles-Henri Sanson. The Swiss and his niece became friendly with the Sanson family, and by the time the Revolution broke out Marie-Anne Sanson was a frequent visitor at Marie Grosholtz's; she enthused over the latter's talent, for Curtius had taught his niece to model in wax and she had become as good as him at it. She was then 29 and still unmarried; tall and slim like her uncle, she had a will of her own and plenty of energy.

In July, 1789, a mob broke into the Waxworks and took away the busts of two heroes of the moment, Necker and the Duc d'Orléans, and carried them in triumph through the streets. Four years later, when the revolutionary Duke had become a suspect, his bust again received attention; but this time from *sans-culottes* who threw bad eggs at it.

Marie Grosholtz cleverly saw how she could profit from the swing in public opinion. She started making wax-models of all the 'public enemies', and soon had queues of people waiting to visit the gallery. As a reward for thus encouraging the change in ideas, the Assembly appointed Curtius to the lucrative post of a commissary with the army in the field; he was sent to Mainz, where his knowledge of German came in very useful.

That much of the story is true; what follows was only rumoured at the time. Marie Grosholtz found difficulty in making her new waxworks faithful reproductions because nearly all the people concerned had leapt into fame or notoriety, and no pictures or drawings of them were available for her to copy. She then had the idea of approaching Charles-Henri and asking him to bring her the heads of his important victims. As he had the responsibility of seeing to their burial, nothing was more simple; he would take or send the severed heads to Marie the evening of the execution, and get them back from her the following morning for burial with the body. She would have ample time during the night to make the mould. The financial terms of the arrangement were agreed upon; and the heads of guillotined 'public enemies' with any claim to temporary fame were taken on a short detour to the Boulevard du Temple before rejoining their trunks in the cemetery.

Another bit of business of Sanson's, again according to popular rumour, concerned the guillotine that had been used on Louis XVI. Far from continuing with it during the Terror, the needy executioner had sold that to Marie Grosholtz; and when people visited her Waxwork Show and gazed at the tableau entitled 'The Death of the Tyrant' they saw Louis XVI under the actual guillotine used on the fatal day.

There are, however, three other versions of what happened to that guillotine, and all are equally doubtful. One account says lots were drawn for it by the 34 towns having a public executioner, and that it went to Auch, in the south-west of France.

Another story is that it was sent out to Devil's Island, the penal colony in French Guiana, and was used on convicts who committed murder there. A third version, however, maintains that it never left Paris and continued to be used during the Terror and for some years afterwards; Charles-Henri merely changed the knife, and kept the one that had cut off the King's head. Years later, Charles-Henri's son or grandson gave this knife to an executioner in the provinces named Roch, and his descendants were still showing it to people at the end of the 19th century.

A variant of the last account was given by Victor Hugo in *Choses Vues*, writing of a meeting he had in the Conciergerie with a prisoner who had been one of Sanson's assistants. According to this man, English visitors to Paris sometimes called at Sanson's house and asked to see the guillotine, regarding the visit as a sort of tourist attraction. Sanson, showing off a little, worked the guillotine for them by using a truss of straw. Hugo quoted the man as saying: 'Nearly all these English visitors asked to see the knife used on Louis XVI. But it had been sold as scrap metal, like all those from the guillotine when they were getting worn. The visitors refused to believe that, and always offered to buy the knife from Sanson. If he had wanted to, he could have sold as many 'Louis XVI knives' as there are 'Voltaire walking-sticks'.'

Whatever the truth about Charles-Henri's unsavoury dealings during the Terror, he certainly continued to demand payment from the public-prosecutor and to brandish the threat of his resignation. Fouquier-Tinville sent an application to the Committee of Public Safety in which, pretending the whole subject was distasteful to him, he made a plea in favour of 'the guillotine which, wholly unpleasant as it is, has its uses and should not be neglected'. The Committee was moved by the public-prosecutor's phrases to order him to pay Sanson a special allowance of 20,000 *livres* — as is proved by the receipt in the Archives Nationales and which is dated 'the thirteenth of Floréal, Second Year of the Republic one and indivisible.' (May 1st, 1794).

Less than three months later, Robespierre and his party were overthrown. On the morning of that day, the Ninth of Thermidor,

Fouquier-Tinville obtained death-sentences on 24 accused persons, at the Palais de Justice. Nothing had been heard there of the violent scenes in the Assembly, which sat at the Tuileries. As the public-prosecutor was leaving his office he bumped into Charles-Henri Sanson and a man named Comtat who worked in the records-office. These two had just arrived, and on their way had seen crowds gathering and heard drums beating; rumours were flying round, something was obviously afoot, Sanson told Fouquier-Tinville. When Charles-Henri learnt there were 24 prisoners to be executed he suggested waiting for a day. 'It would be safer,' he said.

Fouquier thought for a moment. 'No, carry on,' he replied. 'Justice must have its way.' And off he went to his lunch.

At the Conciergerie, Sanson found there were not 24 but 42 prisoners to be 'shortened', the others having been condemned by a different court from the one where Fouquier had prosecuted. Sanson might have ignored these, giving the excuse if Robespierre and his party won the day that he had kept to Fouquier-Tinville's orders. But he did nothing of the kind, and 42 heads fell into the basket.

Meanwhile, at the Conventional Assembly, Robespierre and his friends had been accused and led away under guard. But no prison would accept them, the staff being unaware of what had occurred and refusing to believe it when told. The Robespierre faction, finding themselves free, made their way in twos and threes to the Hôtel de Ville, the headquarters of the Paris Commune which supported Robespierre. There, soldiers under the orders of Hanriot, the commander of the National Guard, prepared to defend the building against troops loyal to the Assembly and commanded by Barras.

Among the latter was Henri Sanson's company. He arrived in the Place de Grève with his two guns, and lined up his men; then awaited orders, along with the other units assembled in the square. Contradictory rumours and reports were going around — the Convention had been dissolved and Robespierre was back in power ... no, he had been proscribed ... Whom should the soldiers obey, Barras or Hanriot? Where did their duty lie?

Just then a high-ranking officer came out of the Town Hall and went up to the first unit-commander he saw. It happened to be Henri Sanson, unfortunately. In a commanding voice, the officer ordered Sanson to go into the Town Hall 'to have his presence checked'. Accompanied by his sergeant-major, Henri obeyed. He said later that he never heard his colonel calling to him not to go.

He was taken into a room where a noisy meeting was taking place and, after signing an order sheet, was told to go with his men and the two guns to the Central Bureau. This administrative office was in the little rue de Jérusalem, between the Sainte Chapelle and the Seine; and its staff remained loyal to Robespierre. Henri Sanson's mission was supposed to be to guard some treasure kept there, but actually he and his small force were intended for the defence of this outpost of the Commune.

Did Captain Sanson accept this mission because of his political opinions? Or did he let himself be taken in by men sharper than he? In any case, through complicity or candour, he led his men away to the Ile de la Cité and placed them in defensive positions around the Central Bureau.

Meanwhile, Barras had captured the Hôtel de Ville. A company of gendarmes burst into the room where Robespierre and his supporters were gathered. Robespierre had his jaw shattered by a bullet; his brother Augustin jumped out of a window and broke his leg.

The following day, the men who had sent so many to the guillotine were themselves executed by it, 21 in all. There were horrible scenes; either the executioner and his assistants had become completely brutalised by all the killings, or else they feared for their lives and wanted to ingratiate themselves with the new masters. The paralytic Couthon was thumped and pulled to try and straighten him on the sliding plank, and finally had to be guillotined with his body askew. Robespierre had a bandage round his shattered jaw; Charles-Henri tore it away, and the victim gave a scream of pain.

People who went into Marie Grosholtz's Waxwork Show the

next day were able to see the dictator's head on a white cushion; it had a shattered jaw and was all bloody, evoking the agonies of the man's last hours. So like the original was it, that some people wondered whether it was a wax copy or the head itself.

Wealthy Marie Grosholtz became suspect, was arrested and put in La Force prison. But before long a friend in high places obtained her release; she then learnt that her uncle had died and left his money and property to her. In 1795 she married François Tussaud, and retired from the public scene for some years. But after Napoleon seized power she appeared in certain social circles, and even managed to get invited to one or two of Josephine's afternoon receptions. Suddenly she heard that Napoleon had told his wife to cease receiving her. Fearing arrest again, Madame Tussaud and her husband took advantage of the temporary peace between the warring powers and crossed to England, taking with them the moulds and waxworks and all the material inherited from Curtius.

The couple settled in London and opened 'Tussaud's Museum' — which became known the world over. Madame Tussaud died in 1850 at the age of 90, and in her turn appeared among the waxworks on show.

The death of Robespierre was the end of the Terror, but for Charles-Henri Sanson it marked the beginning of some days of terrible suspense. Not because he feared having to guillotine Fouquier-Tinville and the judges who had supported Robespierre; he hated them too much to feel any pity for them. But among those recently arrested and awaiting trial was his own son, Henri.

The victors of Thermidor had discovered the order sheet signed by Captain Sanson, among the papers at the Hôtel de Ville. He had left the Central Bureau with his unit after hearing that Barras had won the day, and believing himself above suspicion. But, unfortunately, he had not read the 'order sheet' before signing it; and the wording contained the oath of loyalty to the Commune. His argument that he had gone to defend the Central Bureau in all good faith therefore carried little weight. His signature showed he was on the other side, and he was accused of complicity in the revolt led by Hanriot. He was arrested while at his father's house and taken prisoner to the Conciergerie.

Henri was put in the cell that had been occupied by Marie-Antoinette. He slept in the bed she had slept in, and suffered agonies of suspense as his royal victim had done.

It was an unbearable situation for his parents. They not only feared for their son's life, but if he were condemned his own father would inevitably be called upon to execute him!

Fortunately, the law of Prairial had been abolished, and the accused could again be defended by an advocate. Charles-Henri, for some psychological reason difficult to fathom, went and asked Maître Chauveau-Lagarde to take his son's case. He was the advocate who had so courageously defended Marie-Antoinette at her trial. Now he agreed to defend Henri Sanson.

The day of the trial, Charles-Henri still kept to his usual habits; he went to the Palais de Justice and walked up and down the corridors waiting to know how many he would have to execute. For the first time in his career, though, he was trembling.

He had to wait for three hours; there were 41 people on trial. In the same great room where Chauveau-Lagarde had tried with unfaltering voice to save the Queen from the executioner, he was now endeavouring to save the executioner himself. Witnesses for the defence testified that Henri was a good republican. If he had been before the previous Tribunal he would not have saved his head . . .

'Acquitted!' he cried as he fell into the arms of his father, who found tears coming to his eyes.

The judges had released forty of the accused. One only was waiting for Sanson.

The guillotine, brought back to the Place de Grève, completed the success of the men of Thermidor. The same frantic crowd, the same screeching furies who had watched victims of the Terror die in the Place de la Révolution now applauded the guillotining in front of the Hôtel de Ville of the men who had provided their daily ration of deaths.

'You scoundrel,' Fouquier-Tinville spat at Henri, who was

again assisting his father, 'I expected to send you where you're taking me!'

And to Charles-Henri he said, 'As the prosecutor is condemned, there's no reason for not condemning the executioner, who's just as guilty!'

He had a case, there. If the executioner detested the Terror so much, he could have fled abroad; or given up in protest, and taken his chance. However, by some miracle as in 1790, nobody dared to attack Sanson in 1794. Everlastingly taboo, the executioner of Damiens had survived the sweeping away of the Old Regime, and having guillotined Danton was now surviving the aftermath of the Terror.

The daily round of Charles-Henri and his family was as active as before, but less gory. The pillory and the branding-iron were used more than the guillotine. The pillory was no longer at the Halles, but in the Place de Grève. Every convict, before being sent to hard labour, was branded on the shoulder with the letters T.F. (*Travaux forcés* — hard labour). Murderers and armed robbers sentenced to life imprisonment had the letters T.F.P. In addition, the letters were preceded by a number that varied according to the *département*. That of the Seine *département*, for instance, was 87; so a Parisian sentenced to a term of hard labour bore the mark 87 T.F. for the rest of his life.

In 1795 Charles-Henri and his wife retired to their house at Brie-Comte-Robert; Martin and Charlemagne went off to become executioners at Tours and Provins respectively. Henri Sanson remained alone in Paris to hold the office of public executioner. He was still unmarried, and approaching his thirtieth year. But two or three years later — there is no record of the exact date — he married Marie-Louise Damidot. She was about nine years younger than he, and as she came from a respectable, comfortably-off family must have had a hard struggle to link her destiny with Sanson's. Was it love, self-interest, or gratitude that brought about such an odd union? Marie-Louise was a lively, alert person but there was a sadness in her face reminiscent of the Mona Lisa — at least, that is what her son wrote later.

This son, the Henri-Clément of the 'Memoirs', was born in 1799. His early childhood was spent almost entirely with his grandparents in the Brie, as his mother wanted to keep knowledge of the family occupation from him as long as possible.

The father now had time to take up the healing practised by the earlier Sansons. He prepared the family remedies, the ointments and the herbal mixtures, and ailing people again began calling at the public executioner's house. Did any of them ask for the fat that was reputed 'excellent for rheumatic pains'. Probably not, as hanging was no longer a mode of execution.

Between times, the quack doctor had his official functions to perform. He executed Lesurques (whose innocence was later established) and the band who had attacked the Lyons Mail-coach; he went to Vendôme to guillotine Babeuf and the first disseminators of the doctrine of common wealth. Hardened by the mass killings during the Terror, Henri Sanson worked the guillotine with indifference.

His father occasionally came up from the country and stayed for a short time in Paris. He appeared on the scaffold on impor-tant occasions, when Henri had plotters against the regime to execute. In 1802 he addressed a plea on behalf of condemned women to the First Consul, as mentioned earlier, and which Napoleon ignored.

Executions were still held in the Place de Grève and still drew large crowds. The guillotine was erected in the centre of the square, opposite the main door of the Town Hall, and the Préfet of the Seine, Nicolas Frochot, could see it from his office. Not particularly liking the sight, he asked the magistrates to have the guillotine put somewhere else — in the Place Maubert, on the other side of the river, for instance. But they favoured the tradi-tional site, and Napoleon had to intervene. A compromise was made by moving the guillotine to the side of the square near the river.

The first person to be executed there was a grocer named Trumeau, on March 19th, 1803. He had been found guilty of poisoning his daughter with arsenic. Some years later, fresh revelations proved him to be innocent of the crime. Henri Sanson had got the impression, as he was about to guillotine him, that the man was innocent; and wrote against his name in the register of executions that he kept: 'Another Lesurques.'

The Sansons, through so often seeing how condemned people went to their death, had acquired a sort of psychological intuition. Henri, though, was not nearly so perceptive as his father. But then, Charles-Henri had more experience; no other public executioner had come anywhere near his record number of executions.

During the Consulate he changed his official attire, discarding the frock-coat and tall hat in favour of a jacket and breeches, stockings and buckle-shoes, with a three-cornered hat; and he wore a slender sword at his side. It was in this dress, which had a flavour of the Old Regime, that he directed the most notorious executions during the Consulate — those of Aréna and other plotters against Napoleon, and of the terrorists who tried to blow him up as he rode through Paris.

But when Cadoudal was condemned to death, Charles-Henri gave his age and his ailments as excuse for returning to his country home, and left the execution to his son. No doubt the condemned man seemed too much of a royalist for the executioner of Louis XVI to wish to have him also on his conscience.

By that time (1804) Charles-Henri was approaching his 66th birthday, and his wife was 72. His stomach pains were becoming more frequent, and eventually grew so acute that he felt his end was near. He came back to Paris, to the family house in the rue Neuve-Saint-Jean, but lingered on for almost two years. In June, 1805, he had such a severe attack one day — just before Henri had to guillotine a blind man condemned for attempted murder — that he cried out, clutching at his stomach, 'I wish I were in the blind man's place!'

He got rapidly worse after that. Being with his family and seeing his grandson, Henri-Clément, brought a little joy to his life. Henri said to him one day when the young boy was absent, 'I'll try to get him out of it, to find him a different occupation when he grows up.'

The two women approved; especially Henri's wife, Marie-

Louise, for her parents would have little to do with her since her marriage to the executioner. But Charles-Henri thought otherwise. 'Do nothing of the kind!' he exclaimed. 'If the youngster takes up something different he'll despise all of us!'

Charles-Henri became so ill that he never left his bed. Some months later, on July 4th, 1806, old Marie-Anne realised he would not live through the day and sent for the vicar of St. Laurent's. Religion could be practised openly again since the concordat between Napoleon and the Pope; and the local clergy arrived in force, in procession and with great pomp, at the Sanson house. It was no doubt thought that the executioner of Louis XVI and so many others was in need of every assistance before facing divine wrath.

The seven-year-old Henri-Clément watched the scene with a surprised and curious eye. From a window he saw the choir-boys, the priests and their acolytes reach the house followed by a crowd; and all that made a deeper impression on his young mind than the death of his grandfather.

The funeral service was held two days later. But Charles-Henri could not be buried in the family vault, for the decree abolishing interments within churches was being more strictly enforced. Exceptions were made only for the highest in the land. Marie-Anne had bought a plot in the Montmartre cemetery, and a considerable number of mourners followed the hearse there.

Henri-Clément remembered the funeral in later life, and put down in the 'Memoirs' the chief impression made on his young mind: 'In the district where we lived, the people were quiet and almost sympathetic as the funeral procession went by; but when we got up the hill to Montmartre there were mutterings and talk. I heard someone ask whose funeral it was, and the man replied with an odd sort of look, 'It's the *hangman*.' I felt my father's hand quiver in mine. That was the first time *that word* fell on my ears. Although I didn't know then what it implied, some mysterious instinct made me feel it would be the bane of my life.'

A plain tombstone was put over Charles-Henri's grave, and left blank because his family feared it might be desecrated. The inscription was put on later.

CHAPTER EIGHT

Henri, the Handsome

ALTHOUGH HENRI was 39 and no longer an 'elegant young man' when he succeeded his father officially, he had not lost his handsome looks. His wife was 30, and their son, aged 8, was kept in ignorance of his father's activities. It was unlikely that the boy even knew people were condemned to death. An elderly priest taught him to read and write, some history, and his catechism. There came a day when the old teacher fell ill and had to keep to his bed. Marie-Louise took her son to see him; while she was out of the room for a few minutes the sick old priest, who took a fatherly interest in his young pupil, drew the boy to his bedside.

'Listen, Henri-Clément,' he murmured. 'I'm not long for this world. Your parents will tell you *certain things*, one day. They'll want you to do as they say, and they'll talk about your duty. You'll listen to them if you feel like it. You're free. Men look into their hearts to see what their duty is, and you certainly wouldn't find that one. Remember your old friend's last lesson.'

Henri-Clément was used to an air of mystery hovering about him, and said nothing to his mother of the old priest's words. The man died, and after a time the boy forgot his warning; but a day would come when it would be vividly recalled to him.

His grandmother, Marie-Anne, had no wish to go back to the house at Brie-Comte-Robert; the place reminded her too much of her husband's physical sufferings. So Henri sold it, and bought another house for her, at Brunoy, in the Marne valley, because it was nearer to Paris and there was a school in the town. Henri-Clément went to live there with his grandmother, and started to attend the school. They were using the name of Longval — Henri had bought the house in that name, too — so young Henri-Clément was accepted by his school-fellows as one of themselves.

He did not ask his parents the reason for being called Longval — a youngster of 8 or 9 still trusts his father and mother.

However, his grandmother never allowed him to bring a school-friend home, nor to go to anyone's house. He was too young to be upset by this, certainly to be mystified by it. His parents came to see him on Sundays, arriving by post-chaise in the morning and returning to Paris in the evening.

When he was 11 and due to make his First Communion, his parents took him back to Paris with them; the ceremony was to be held in St. Laurent's, where his father and grandfather had made their First Communions. For the first time, the lad objected; he would have preferred to remain with the school-fellows with whom he had been attending catechism classes. At his parents' home his surprise grew when he was told that instead of joining the procession of local First Communicants he was to have a private ceremony. His parents made out this was a special favour, a privilege not given to everyone. 'We're not ordinary folk,' said his mother. He felt bewildered by such treatment, and yet was aware of something peculiar going on.

Henri-Clément made his First Communion in one of the side-chapels, at eight in the morning; as he came out of church with his parents he saw the procession of boys and girls entering and going down the nave, dressed in their special new clothes. He was so struck by this dissimilarity that he suddenly remembered the words of the old priest and felt a need to talk about them. He questioned his parents and his grandmother, but all three gave evasive answers.

Two days later he returned to Brunoy with his grandmother, and started school again.

His father's job was no longer on the same scale as in the previous decade. People condemned for political crimes were now shot; the public executioner only got common criminals. This increased the general ignominy attached to his functions.

Among the despicable wretches Henri had to guillotine was one whose trial received much publicity — a woman by the name of Manette Bonhourt, but who called herself Auguste. This masculine name is explained by the fact that she committed all her murders dressed as a man. She had been seduced when a girl and then been deserted by the man, and had sworn revenge on the hated sex; to punish one man, she drew many others into her frightful trap.

She was still young and pretty; and when she stood on a corner giving the glad eye, with a top-hat perched on her blond curls, wearing a man's jacket that fitted snugly to her rounded figure and tight white breeches that showed off her legs, she did not have long to wait to pick up some man interested in the novelty. Then she would take him to an hotel — though never the same one — and ask for drinks to be sent up to the room. While the man has his back turned for a moment she dropped a sleeping-pill into his glass. When he fell asleep, she slipped out of the bed and got a hammer she had kept hidden under her jacket. A neat blow on the left temple — always on the same spot and always fatal — killed the unfortunate fellow. She spent the rest of the night by the corpse and left the hotel in the morning, though not without first lifting the dead man's purse. 'I've got a few errands to do,' she would say to the hall-porter. 'Don't wake my husband, he's still asleep. I'll be back at midday.'

Over the years, Manette Bonhourt committed a score of murders in this way. Each time, she changed afterwards into the dress of her own sex and disappeared for a while. Nobody could remember what her face was like, because her costume drew all attention. Fouché's police never managed to get on her track; until one of them, not knowing who he was dealing with, went with her to an hotel. But when a peculiar drowsiness came over him after having a drink, he began to realise who she was; and, with an effort, collecting his remaining senses, he shouted for help. Servants came running, and found pretty Manette with the hammer in her hand.

She admitted everything when arrested, confessing to all the murders she had committed, though she was not sure of the exact number. She seemed proud of showing *the men* questioning her the extent of the revenge she had taken. She even confessed to murdering a girl whom she suspected of having identified her.

At her trial, the prosecution replied to her excuse — a natural hatred of men — by reminding the court that she had robbed her victims. She retorted that vengeance uses every means, pilfering as well as greater crimes. There were some credulous people who took her part and pitied the *poor unfortunate woman*. She was condemned to death, and appealed against the verdict. Instead of knowing the result of her appeal at the end of six weeks, as was usual then, she had to wait two years; campaigns in her favour and approaches to Napoleon on her behalf caused her execution to be repeatedly delayed.

At the Conciergerie the prisoner was admired by her jailers. She was always calm and smiling, and looked prettier than ever. Although wearing woman's clothes, she kept her male attire in her cell. 'I shall put it on again to go to the scaffold,' she said. 'I shall die in the clothes I took my revenge in.'

Henri Sanson and his assistants went to collect her on May 16th, 1808. And they did in fact find her dressed as when she had committed her crimes. They cut off her fair locks and tied her hands without any lamentation on her part; nor did she scorn or revile them, but conducted herself in a gracious, feminine way.

Executions then took place either at nine in the morning or, what was more usual, at four in the afternoon. The day before, street-criers went round selling a broadsheet with the verdict and sentence for a *sou*, and announcing the morrow's *show*. This deplorable custom dated back to the time of Louis XIV, and had survived the Revolution. However, the crowds that gathered in the Place de Grève were kept in check by the police and behaved more seemly than in the past. People who lived in the square were no longer allowed to let their windows.

It was, therefore, a well-conducted crowd that watched Manette Bonhourt arrive in Sanson's cart. A priest was standing next to her, exhorting her to have courage; she had more than he had. Her graciousness and humble attitude did not diminish the infamy of her crimes, but did arouse admiration. On the scaffold she showed great calmness. 'Don't you think,' she said to Henri, 'that it's a pity to cut off such a pretty head?'

Her composure was broken only when she noticed the prepon-
derance of men in the crowd nearest the scaffold. 'The cowards,
the base, vicious lot!' she exclaimed in a burst of rage. 'They'd
rather have seen me stripped for a whipping!'

For the whip was still used. This ancient punishment had been
revived a few years earlier in an attempt to intimidate the
increasing numbers of counterfeiters. In September, 1802, it was
inflicted on three men and a woman. It was not only painful but
humiliating too, as the culprits were stripped to the waist.

During the Empire there were more false coins and counterfeit
notes in circulation than ever. The Legislative Body set up a
'special criminal court' to try to eliminate the scourge; it sat
without a jury and had power to pass sentence of death on
convicted forgers. This class of criminal became prominent
among Henri Sanson's clientele.

The most numerous were those whose sentences included a
period in the pillory. Their frequency can be judged by examining
the newspapers of the day. Almost every issue of the *Journal de
l'Empire*, for instance, contained in its Paris columns announcements such as: 'A man named François Romain has been sentenced
to six years' hard labour and to be stood in the pillory for fraud.'
'At the Assizes, Jacques Marquis was sentenced to eight years'
hard labour, to be branded and stood in the pillory for two
hours, for fraudulent conversion.' 'A master-baker named Poussin
has been sentenced to three hours in the pillory for destroying
four notes worth 3,500 francs, by swallowing them.'

And here is an item which, though less delectable than the last,
reported the end of a case that had set all Paris talking:

'At eleven this morning the widow Morin and her daughter,
Angélique Delaporte, were brought from the Conciergerie prison
to the square in front of the Palais de Justice and were stood in
the pillory for one hour, before a great crowd that extended into
the streets leading to the square. The demeanour of both was in
keeping with their social position. It was noticed that when the
executioner released the girl, the first use she made of her hands
was to raise them to the heavens.'

The date was February 18th, 1812. The mother and her daughter had been victimised by a scoundrel named Ragouleau, who had lent them money to buy an hotel. But the loan agreement contained a complicated clause by which Madame Morin, who knew little about financial matters, had mortgaged the hotel to Ragouleau; and, finding herself unable to keep up the annual payments, she was forced to quit the hotel yet still owed him the original sum.

She and her daughter swore to have their revenge. They rented an isolated house on the northern outskirts of Paris and asked Ragouleau to go there to collect some of the money owing to him. When he arrived, the two produced pistols and threatened to shoot him if he did not sign a receipt that the debt had been paid in full. But he got away, neither mother nor daughter daring to fire on him, and went and told the police.

The two were arrested and brought to trial, charged with attempted murder. Their defence was that they had had no intention of shooting Ragouleau, that they only meant to frighten him into signing the receipt. The daughter, Angélique, was only 16. 'Do you think I could kill a man at my age?' she pleaded through her tears.

In those days, they could have been sentenced to death; instead, they each got twenty years' hard labour and an hour in the pillory. All Paris pitied the mother and daughter; Sanson asked their pardon when he put them in the pillory. At the end of the hour they were taken away to St. Lazare prison to begin their sentence. They had to serve it in full; when they came out, the mother was 60 and the daughter 37.

When Henri-Clément was nearly 13, he and his grandmother left Brunoy for Paris. It was time for the lad to be made aware of his father's functions, to get used to the idea that one day he would have to put a Madame Morin in the pillory, whip a forger, and guillotine a Manette Bonhourt.

Nothing was said to him straight away, though. His family counted on his insight and sagacity; he would notice the comings and goings of the assistants with the cart, perhaps see the guillotine in its shed; he would gradually realise the significance of it all, without difficult explanations having to be made, without any sudden shock — the Sansons had always acted in this way with their young sons, ever since the first Charles.

In the meantime, Henri Sanson sent his son to a school run by a Monsieur Michel, in the rue du Faubourg St. Denis. The name of Longval served as a screen, as at Brunoy; but Henri thought it best to tell Monsieur Michel, in confidence, his true identity. The headmaster was confused at first, but agreed to take the boy.

Henri-Clément went there each day at seven, had his lunch — then eaten at ten o'clock — at the school, continued lessons in the afternoon, did his homework in class, and returned to the house at six in the evening.

A school-friend came back with him one evening, and Henri-Clément quite naturally asked his friend into the house. When they met Sanson, Henri-Clément was surprised to see his father's face darken and to hear him speak to the young friend so coldly that the latter went off at once.

At school next day the friend would not speak to Henri-Clément, nor would the other boys have anything to do with him. After a week of this, the unhappy, puzzled lad, finding himself alone in the classroom with the boy he considered responsible for him being sent to Coventry, exclaimed: 'What's the matter? Why have you stopped being friends with me? Is it because my father was so unkind to you?'

The other boy turned his back and made no reply. But Henri-Clément persisted, and his schoolfellow began drawing something on a sheet of paper. Henri-Clément was too agitated to notice what the other was doing. 'Why won't you tell me?' he cried.

The boy silently handed him the paper. Henri-Clément saw a rough drawing of a guillotine, with the words *Tuus pater carnifex*. He quickly translated it in his head — 'Your father is the hangman.' He gave a horrified cry. Everything suddenly became clear — the mysterious words of the old priest, the First Communion held almost in secret, the use of the name Longval.

He rushed out of the classroom with the sheet of paper, ran down the stairs and into the street. A few minutes later he reached home, breathless and in tears, burst into the room where his mother was and showed her the paper.

She did not deny what was on it, but tried to console her son, making vague answers or evading direct replies to his pointed questions. It was his grandmother, old Marie-Anne, who bluntly confirmed what Henri-Clément's class-mate had asserted.

'Yes, it is indeed your father who executes convicted criminals,' she told him when she came in. 'Our family has had this dreaded honour for a hundred and fifty years. We were waiting until you had reached an age to understand its stern duties, before telling you.'

But how had the school-friend known the real identity of Henri-Clément's father? No doubt he had told his parents, on returning home, of the strange and chilly reception; and in reply to their questions had described the house. And they, knowing the district well, had exclaimed, 'But that's the hangman's house!'

The boy had perhaps thought he was not revealing anything to Henri-Clément, that the Sansons did not hide from their son the strange position of the family.

From that day, young Sanson's life took a different turn; he left the school, and instead his father started to adapt his mind to an acceptance of his own functions. It was no easy task. Henri began by telling his son of his own fears when a lad; that at the age of 13 he had been going to the Place de Grève with his father for twelve months.

'My uncle Charlemagne could tell you about it. The tears I shed in his arms! He was younger than my father and understood me better. I won't make you do what I had to; you can come on the scaffold when you want to. And if you want to earn a living differently, you're free to try! But I warn you — you'll never manage it. Our name closes all doors against us; people turn from us in horror. Even at school — you've had that sad experience. It's impossible for a Sanson to earn his living other than the way his fathers did before him.'

Henri was not exaggerating. And the experience of Louis-Gabriel Sanson a few years later proved his words.

This Louis-Gabriel was a son of Charlemagne Sanson, who had returned to Provins after the Terror and taken up his office of public executioner there. In 1814, at the age of 23, Louis-Gabriel left his parents and went off to Troyes, the county town of the Aube, to try and begin a new life. He became apprenticed to a locksmith, and soon married a young woman of Troyes. By 1819 they had three children, and Louis-Gabriel had started up his own workshop. But although an honest workman and good at his job, he had few customers; his name kept them away. He fell on bad times. His mother, by then a widow, sent him some money now and then; but she had only a small pension of 400 francs a year. In any case, this help came to an end in 1823, when she died; and Louis-Gabriel then asked permission of the municipality of Provins to move with his family into the house his mother had occupied, which belonged to the town. It was in a narrow lane that descends the hill topped by Caesar's Tower, and was known locally as 'The Hangman's House'. The door had been painted red, to warn people away from it.[1]

Louis-Gabriel received support for his request from the Préfet. 'This family is cut off from the rest of society by the functions exercised by the late father,' wrote the Préfet, 'and although the conduct of its members is irreproachable they find themselves in a state of indigence and neglect.' The municipality of Provins allowed Louis-Gabriel to move into the house with his wife and children. But where did he get any money from? There is a tale that he was offered his father's place, but replied he'd rather starve first. Apparently he was permitted, to the great indignation of the local people, to collect a tax on games of skittles played in open public spaces. Previous to Charlemagne Sanson's original appointment as executioner at Provins, in the latter part of the 18th century, a public executioner named Ferey had received the modest amount this tax brought in.

However, in 1813 young Henri-Clément could not foresee what his cousin would try to do a year later and how it would turn out, and he followed his father's advice. As all doors were closed

---

[1]) The house is still standing, and is visited by tourists.

to the son of a public executioner, then that was what he would become.

The office was again well-paid. The decrease in the number of death sentences allowed a reduction in the number of assistants. Henri Sanson now had only two, yet received the same salary as had his father. Moreover, his expenses were refunded; and as they were never checked, he added something on. He supplemented his income, too, by continuing with his quack medicine and, in addition, some minor surgery. Altogether, so much money was coming in that Marie-Louise and her mother-in-law were able to give considerably to the charities of the parish.

Although sick people hesitated a little to go and consult the public executioner, Henri had quite a good number of clients. If need be, some asked him to visit them at home. The executioner's reputation as a healer and quack-doctor only diminished as his official functions grew less; when the guillotine was no longer in daily use, people began to forget about him. And, too, as the regulations on the practice of medicine became more stringent, unqualified healers were obliged to keep quiet about their activities.

But they still flourished in the early years of the 19th century, and Henri Sanson was one much in demand. According to an unconfirmed story, the celebrated surgeon, Dupuytren, sent some patients to him.

Henri tried to teach his son the elements of his healing art, which was based entirely on practical experience; but Henri-Clément was not very keen on these lessons. To his mind, they represented a step nearer a future he had accepted but which he dreaded. 'I'll never have the courage to guillotine anyone,' he told his grandmother.

'You must,' the old lady replied. And urged him to pluck up courage and go with his father to an execution.

It was some time before the youngster made up his mind, and then France was shaken by an unexpected event. Napoleon escaped from Elba, landed on the southern coast of France, and made for Paris gathering troops on the way. The Emperor reached the capital on March 20th, 1815, the very day that Henri-

Clément was to have attended his first execution. The condemned man was an ex-lieutenant named Dautun; he had been dismissed from the army when Louis XVIII returned to the Bourbon throne and, being in want, had killed two people for their money. When the city magistrates heard of the welcome being given to Napoleon they decided to postpone the execution until the 29th, not wishing to be responsible for such a gory spectacle on the day the Emperor entered Paris.

Henri-Clément gave a sigh of relief — there were still nine days to go, and in the meantime perhaps Napoleon would reprieve the ex-lieutenant. But it is unlikely that the Emperor ever heard of the matter. Young Sanson's hopes faded; and on the 29th he went with his father to collect Dautun from prison.

'You're going to guillotine an innocent man!' cried the ex-lieutenant when they entered his cell. He continued to proclaim his innocence on the way to the Place de Grève. 'I am innocent!' he exclaimed when on the scaffold. 'Is this the way for a soldier to die?'

His protests had a worse effect on Henri-Clément than hearing the knife fall; at that moment, he turned his eyes away. At 16, the executioner's son realised the full horror of the future awaiting him, and he returned home in tears.

A few months later he married. His bride, Virginie-Emilie Lefébure, was a year older than him, so that the combined ages of the newly-married couple only amounted to 33. The Lefébures did not belong to the confraternity. They had visited the Sanson house occasionally, possibly to consult Henri as a healer on their daughter's behalf, and Henri-Clément had met the girl. Was it a case of love at first sight? That is difficult to believe. A girl of 17 is usually more mature than a lad of the same age, and is far more likely to develop a passion for a man older than herself than to fall in love with a youngster — that is an accepted psychological fact. Did, then, Henri-Clément — who in later years was always running after women — treat the girl with more intimate attention than his father prescribed for her? Was he obliged to 'do the right thing' and marry her? The fact that his marriage corres-

ponded with his decision to assist his father as executioner gives
support to such belief — that the latter was a sudden outcome of
the former. Finding himself unexpectedly with a wife and obliged
to earn a living, he finally accepted the family destiny. Because of
this marriage, Henri Sanson was able to overcome his son's
distaste, and to fall in with Charles-Henri's last wishes — which
had been summed up in the phrase: 'If the youngster takes up
something different he'll despise all of us!'

So another person came to live at the Sanson house in the rue
Neuve-Saint-Jean. Two others had been given a home there only
a short time before Henri-Clément's wedding — a Madame Collet
de Charmoy and her daughter, Mademoiselle Lexcellent. The first
was in her seventies and the widow of a public executioner at
Amiens whose sister had married Martin Sanson, the public
executioner at Tours and uncle of Henri; the other was in her
forties and was Madame de Charmoy's daughter by a previous
marriage. Both were without any financial resources, and so most
grateful for the charitable aid of their remote relative, for the
solidarity that still existed in the tribe.

Another widow, Marie-Anne, was enjoying a quiet old age in
this growing household. She had a servant specially to look after
her, who slept in the adjoining room and whom the old grandmother could call by pulling at a bell-rope. But one morning — it
was October 24th, 1817 — when the servant went into Marie-
Anne's bedroom, having heard nothing during the night, she
found the old widow had died peacefully in her sleep, like a lamp
run out of oil. At the age of 84 she had at last gone to join her
husband . . .

But where was she buried? Her name is the only one missing
from the tombstone in Montmartre cemetery, and the registers
contain no record of her burial there. Why did Henri not have
her buried alongside her husband? The answer can very likely be
found in the political atmosphere of the time. The Restoration
Government had passed a law banishing the regicides; 206
members of the Convention who had voted the death of Louis
XVI came under it, and a special court was ready to sentence to
death any who remained in France. No mention was made of the

executioners of Louis XVI and Marie-Antoinette, but Henri
Sanson feared that at any moment attention might be called to
him and his family. He kept as quiet as possible, forbidding any
of his family to leave the house, and only going out himself when
his functions obliged him to. At the time his old mother died, the
royalist excesses of the 'White Terror' were sweeping across
France, and there was a flurry of panic in the Sanson house.

Charles-Henri's funeral had drawn a crowd of curious and
hostile onlookers. Would the same occur at his widow's funeral,
and thereby provoke 'the avengers of Louis XVI' to take action
against the Sansons? Henri probably thought so; and that may be
the reason for Marie-Anne Sanson being buried secretively,
without any tolling of church bells, in a place which was perhaps
discovered by the Communards of 1871 ... but that will come
later.

In any case, Henri Sanson need not have feared for himself and
his family. The public executioner was as useful to the royalists
as he had been to their adversaries, and he remained an untouch-
able. The royal courts sent him three 'parricides' — three men
found guilty of plotting to overthrow Louis XVIII, 'the father of
the people.' They were condemned to be guillotined after first
having their hand chopped off — this ancient punishment being
restored to the penal code by the political jackals.

Henri-Clément went with his father to the execution, but
refused to go on the scaffold. He remained at the foot of the
steps, hearing all the grisly proceedings and the crowd shout
'Vive le Roi!' as the heads fell — just as other crowds used to
shout 'Vive la République!' on similar occasions.

But a day came when the young man had to take charge of
proceedings himself. It was in January, 1819, and his father was
ill with pleurisy, unable to leave his bed. Henri-Clément went to
the prison with the assistants to collect the condemned man, a
soldier named Foulard who had robbed and murdered two
women. He and his executioner were of the same age — 20. The
abbé Montès, a priest well-known and respected for his solace
and administrations to condemned prisoners, got into the cart
with Foulard.

'Are you taking your father's place?' the priest said to Henri-Clément. 'Much courage is needed for such tasks. Our aims are opposite, yours and mine, but our ways run alongside. You represent the justice of men, and I the mercy of God. May I make a request in His name? Do not give the signal until this poor boy has uttered the words, "I deliver my soul into Your hands, O God." '

Henri-Clément promised, and passed the instruction to Fauconnier, his chief assistant; for he still could not force himself to go on the scaffold. He stayed below, legalizing the execution by his presence. At the sound of the knife falling, and the head dropping with a thud into the leather sack, Henri-Clément was seen to grip the handrail of the steps for support.

His father's illness lasted a long time, and he was obliged to continue replacing him. Habit becoming a second nature, Henri-Clément finally acquired the necessary courage and firmness. By the time Henri was completely recovered, his son could perform the functions with the efficiency of their forefathers — but with an obvious loathing of the office. That was something new in the Sanson line. All the same, during his lifetime he was to execute, sometimes assisting his father, sometimes in sole charge, a total of 111 people. (A small number compared with the executions carried out by each of his forefathers.)

He guillotined Louvel, the assassin of the Duc de Berry. A kindly gesture by Henri-Clément was pounced on by some historical writers as supporting their contention that Louvel was none other than Louis XVII, the Dauphin imprisoned in the Temple and whose fate was even then one of the enigmas of history.

The day that Henri-Clément and his father went to the Conciergerie to collect Louvel there was a cold wind blowing and rain falling. When Louvel saw what the weather was like, he hesitated at the door and asked for his hat. Although only 37, he was completely bald, and feared he might catch cold. This was just the time to worry about that! Condemned persons were always taken in the cart bareheaded, but through custom and not because of any rule. Henri-Clément looked at Louvel's shiny pate. 'What's he want — his headgear?' he said to one of the assistants. 'Go and get it for him, then.'

Fauconnier went back and fetched Louvel's hat, and clapped it on his head for him, as his hands were tied.

But writers unaware of this detail, and knowing only that Louvel went to the guillotine with his hat on, presumed that Louis XVIII had given orders for this to be allowed — and took it as a proof of the royal origin of the condemned man, whose *uncle* could obviously not let him go bareheaded to his death.

Henri-Clément was helping his father, too, on September 20th, 1822, when four young men were guillotined for plotting against the monarchy. They were all n.c.os who, while in garrison at La Rochelle, had joined an extremist organization. Their case had aroused much interest, and became known as that of 'The Four Sergeants of La Rochelle'. Like Louvel, they wanted an end to the Bourbons; but unlike him, they had not killed anyone.

All four died bravely, showing a courage on the scaffold that astounded Henri-Clément. Each of them refused the administrations of the *abbé* Montès, and cried *'Vive la République!'* as the knife fell. The last of the four, Bories, even made a short speech — repeating the action, peculiarly enough, formerly made by Louis XVI. He slipped from the grasp of the assistants and strode to the edge of the scaffold. Unlike the martyred King, this martyr for Liberty was not interrupted by a roll of drums, although the authorities had placed troops six-deep between the scaffold and the crowd.

'My brothers!' Bories shouted to them. 'If I weep, it is not for myself, but for my poor comrades whose blood has just been spilt before my eyes! In giving our blood, we leave you to avenge us. Remember our last wish — Long live Liberty!'

He was listened to in religious silence. Some of the soldiers fell to their knees, and women fainted away.

The Sansons and their assistants took the four corpses to Montparnasse cemetery, to the plot where executed persons were buried. In the years to come, each time a similar task took Henri-Clément to the cemetery he often noticed a woman near the grave of the four sergeants. She had been Bories's fiancée, and went every day to put flowers on the grave. Henri-Clément would raise his hat whenever he saw her, but she never gave any acknowledgment. With the passage of the years she became bent and frail. Then the public authorities decided to have executed criminals buried at Clamart, just outside Paris, and Henri-Clément saw her no more. In 1864 he read in the newspaper that she had died in hospital.

In the years following the execution of the four sergeants, Henri and his son had common criminals to guillotine. There were also culprits to be put in the pillory, among them an escaped convict — who had to be branded as well — and an army officer, a general in fact, who was being sent to prison for repeated bigamy, and a priest convicted of raping a little girl, though he was later proved to be innocent of the crime.

During this time, the number of public executioners in the regions around Paris was being reduced; and consequently the two Sansons occasionally operated outside the capital, at Versailles and as far afield as Beauvais and Compiègne.

In 1830 the July Revolution brought the Orléans branch to the throne, in the person of Louis-Philippe, the bourgeois King. The old regime that the Bourbons had mistakenly tried to restore was finally swept away. Charles X was in exile, his Ministers in prison, and Marshal Marmont, who had commanded the troops against the rioters, was languishing somewhere in Austria.

But the Sansons? — Henri and his son, who had executed the four sergeants and many others who had tried to bring down the Bourbons — the Sansons were still there in office. As in 1789, and after the Terror, the avenging stream swirled around them and passed on. They could have pleaded in their defence, like a juryman of the *Tribunal Révolutionnaire*, that they were but obeying orders. Nevertheless, a revolution is a blind thing and so many innocent and harmless people get killed as a result that the repeated escape of the Sansons leaves one amazed.

To Henri and his son, the upheavals of 1830 made no difference; their public life and family existence continued as before.

Henri-Clément and his wife Virginie had had three children; the first, a boy, had not lived long, but the other two, both girls, were growing up and learning music and dancing. They played Gluck and Mozart on their great-grandfather's harpsichord, one made by Schmidt, the inventor of the guillotine. Poor girls! The elder was in her early 'teens, and soon it would be time to think of marrying her ... Had she and her sister got to marry public executioners? Virginie felt almost glad at times that the boy had died. The family office would very likely end with Henri-Clément. It was not something to be held out as an inducement to her daughters' suitors!

The family was too well known in the neighbourhood, and Virginie suggested a move would be in the best interests of her daughters. Henri and Marie-Louise agreed; besides, they no longer needed such a large house. Madame Collet de Charmoy was dead, and her daughter had gone into a convent-home; with the changing times, the assistants no longer lodged with the public executioner. Only the family itself remained — Henri and his wife, their son and daughter-in-law and their two girls, and two servants; eight persons in all.

There was not even need of a house — an apartment would do! And to keep their identity hidden — still thinking of the young girls — they would rent a stable for the cart and horses, and a shed for the guillotine, some little distance away.

They began to look for accommodation to let. But each time a landlord was approached he wanted to know Henri's name and occupation ... and expressed his regret that there was nothing available. With the executioner of Marie-Antoinette as a tenant ...!

Finally, in despair, Henri bought a smaller house in the rue des Marais-Saint-Martin, at number 31.A. It was in the same district as where the family was already living, but at least they were moving to another street; and a house-painter let Henri a building, on the nearby Quai de Valmy, for stabling the horses and storing the equipment.

No sooner had the Sansons moved into their new house than everybody in the neighbourhood knew who they were. It was their fate to be followed everywhere by their grisly renown. When a housewife passed their windows and heard the piano being played she would mutter with a grimace, 'That's the hangman's daughters playing a Requiem.'

It was at about this time that the government, as though wishing to help the Sansons fade into the background, decreed that no more executions were to take place in front of the Hôtel de Ville, in the square where so much blood had been shed since medieval times. The terrible spectacle was moved from the centre of Paris, and in the future the guillotine was set up when necessary by the St. Jacques Barrier, at the southern limits of the city, in a district which then had such a bad name that people would hesitate to venture into it.[1]

For six months, however, Sanson was not required to set up the guillotine. The abolition of the death penalty was a subject very much under discussion. It was being debated in the Chamber of Deputies and in the Senate; newspapers had taken sides, and books were written around it.

In 1832 Victor Hugo brought out a new edition of his book, 'The Last Day of a Condemned Man', which he had first published anonymously three years earlier. He had been inspired to write it by the sight of a crowd waiting to see a public execution and making a day out of it. Some time later, passing by the Hôtel de Ville, he had seen the executioner trying out the guillotine, greasing it and making sure the knife worked properly; this rehearsal seemed as ghastly and odious a thing to Hugo as the act itself. The following day he had started to write 'The Last Day of a Condemned Man', and had finished it in three weeks.

In the preface to the 1832 edition Hugo stated in passionate terms that the book was in fact meant as an attack on the death penalty. He recalled the parliamentary debates on the subject, and referred to Sanson: 'The *bourreau* was most alarmed. When he heard our law-makers were talking of humanity, benevolence

---

[1] The guillotine, when erected, stood where the entrance to the St. Jacques Métro station is today, at the point where the rue de la Tombe-Issoire crosses the Boulevard St. Jacques.

towards mankind, and progress, he thought he was finished. The wretch hid himself away; he crouched beneath his guillotine, unable to face this glorious daylight... No one saw him for six months. He gave no sign of life. But he gradually became reassured in his dim hideout. He had cocked an ear towards Parliament and not heard his name being mentioned any more. There were no more of those great resounding words that had alarmed him so much... Parliament was dealing with other business, with matters of grave social interest, a lane through a village, a subsidy for the Opéra-Comique...

'He was forgotten about, and so the cutter of heads grew easier in his mind. He looked out, took a step or two from his hole, like some mouse in La Fontaine's fables, and then risked coming right out from below his scaffold...

'Yes, for six months some unhappy captives had had their sufferings increased, through being given a taste for life again. And then, without rhyme or reason, without quite knowing why, *for the pleasure* of it, one fine morning the respite was ended and all those human creatures were coldly marked for cutting down.'

Hugo's romantic exaggeration nevertheless contained the truth; for six months from the autumn of 1831 several condemned prisoners had deluded themselves with wild hopes, only to meet with a terrible awakening.

Taking up Fouquier-Tinville's words on the scaffold, Hugo classed the public-prosecutor and the public executioner together. What was the latter but a man who earnt his living by bringing others to the guillotine? After fulminating against the guillotine and what it represented, for twenty pages, Hugo concluded by writing: 'In the past, the social structure had three supports — the priest, the King, the hangman. Some time ago a voice cried, "The gods are departing!" Lately, another voice was raised and cried, 'The Kings are departing!' It is time for a third voice to be raised and say, "The hangman is departing!" '

But the hangman did not depart. He set up his guillotine again to execute an ex-convict and murderer named Saint-Clair. The Chamber of Deputies had voted in favour of abolishing the death penalty, but the Upper House had refused to give its support.

Nevertheless a law which was passed on April 28th, 1832, dealt a severe blow to the confraternity of public executioners. The pillory and the branding-iron were done away with, and a clause permitting the pleading of extenuating circumstances was introduced into the penal code. As a result, the number of public executioners and their assistants in the whole of France was reduced from 86 to 20 or so. Nearly all the Sansons, descendants of the nine brothers and sisters of Charles-Henri, found themselves dismissed from office. For them, the relentless family destiny had come to an end. *Monsieur de Paris*, though, remained in office.

Whether they were grieved or pleased by these events, they owed it to the campaign worked up by Victor Hugo. He had followed up his book, 'The Last Day of a Condemned Man', by publishing 'Claude Gueux', the true story of a criminal of that name, in the *Revue de Paris;* and he continued to attack the death penalty in a number of newspapers. Many years later he was to return to the subject with his famous book, *Les Misérables,* which shows how Mother Poverty begets Son Crime.

A different point of view was expressed in print by an official with a greater experience of the world of crime — L-M Moreau-Christophe, who was Inspector-general of prisons. In his opinion, it was rather crime that led to poverty. He maintained it was the lack of education that caused men to commit robbery and murder; if they escaped being caught by the police, it was by entering the underworld and leading a life that soon became one of poverty — and to get out of that, another crime was committed. A vicious circle was set up, and could only be broken by the guillotine. If all poverty could suddenly be done away with, wrote Moreau-Christophe, that would not cause crime to disappear from the face of the earth. He supported his theme by quoting figures which showed thefts of foodstuffs to amount to only one-percent of all the theft committed in France; and bread was stolen least of all. The real causes of crime were therefore not poverty and hunger, but brutal urges, lack of education, absence of all restraint, and immorality.

In later years, Moreau-Christophe published several books,

one of them — *Le Monde des Coquins* — being in the nature of a reply to *Les Misérables*. In it, referring to the law of April, 1832, that had brought in extenuating circumstances, Moreau-Christophe wrote: 'That is just right for knaves, whose trade thereby pays better and becomes less risky. Does the author of *Les Misérables*, who thinks our penal laws are still too severe, want to make that trade even more attractive?'

In any case, in 1832 the debates in Parliament on the death penalty, and the publicity given by Hugo's campaign, put public executioners in the news. And one result of this was that English visitors to Paris began calling at Henri Sanson's house in the rue des Marais.

The first of such callers were brought by Benjamin Appert, who had been made a member of the Royal Society of French Prisons for his philanthropic works. A teacher by profession, he had approached the War Ministry about the great number of soldiers who were unable to read or write, and in 1818 he had been given the task of opening classes for every regiment. In a few years, a hundred thousand soldiers ceased to be illiterate, thanks to Appert's devoted work.

In 1822 he had been accused of helping two political prisoners to escape, and was himself sent to jail for a time. This experience caused him to try and improve the lot of prisoners. He published a treatise on elementary education for them, and for five years edited a monthly called *Le Journal des Prisons*. In 1832 he brought out the first of the four volumes of his work, *Bagnes, Prisons, et Criminels*. His renown opened all administrative doors to him; he was invited to dinner by magistrates and Ministers, and even by Louis-Philippe. It was through Appert that the guillotine was transferred from the Place de Grève to the St. Jacques Barrier. He also made representations for the punishment of exposition to the public to be abolished — the pillory itself having recently been done away with — but was unsuccessful.

Appert had often met and questioned the two Sansons at the Palais de Justice. These interviews were rather repugnant to him, but it was all on behalf of public welfare. In social life the ex-teacher was known as a gay companion with a dry wit, and a lover of good food and wine. Philanthropy does not bar a man from being joyful; on the contrary.

He sometimes made bantering remarks to Henri Sanson and his son over their insistence on calling the guillotine 'the machine'. Their queer notion of honour caused them to regard the official term as lacking in respect towards them.

One day Benjamin Appert had three distinguished Englishmen to lunch at his house — Lord Durham, Sir John Bowring, and Lord Ellice, the Minister for War. The conversation turned on the Sansons and the likely effect on them of the debates then taking place in the Chamber of Deputies. It was then that the three asked Appert to take them to visit the Sansons at home. They pressed him so much that he gave way, and after lunch the four set out in a carriage.

Henri Sanson's wife opened the door to the visitors and ushered them into her husband's office. Henri got up from his chair, taking off the cotton bonnet that — as Appert later wrote in his Memoirs — 'covered his large and lofty bald head'. On the walls of the room, to the Englishmen's astonishment, were hanging a large number of religious prints, arranged around portraits of all the Sansons since the first Charles. Old swords of justice with dented blades — dented from use on noble victims — were laid out on velvet. The sounds of a piano were coming from another room.

Henri asked his visitors to be seated. The three Englishmen accepted the invitation, but Appert remained standing. His host had offered him the last remaining armchair with the words, spoken quite naturally: 'That was my father's. He liked it very much, and spent all night in it sometimes, during the Terror, when he couldn't get to sleep in bed.' The thought of sitting in such a refuge did not at all appeal to the philanthropist. Henri affected not to notice; he turned to the other three, and told them some of his reminiscences.

Lord Durham asked if he could 'see how the machine worked'.

'Certainly,' Henri replied. 'I'll use it on some trusses of straw. But that's not possible today; my assistants are doing some repairs to it. You'll have to come back another day, my lord.'

'Would next Saturday be convenient?'
'As you wish.'
The visitors took their departure.

On the Saturday, Lord Ellice and Sir John went straight to the Sanson house together, while Lord Durham first called to collect Appert. The two latter were followed by a number of other carriages, for Durham had spoken of his visit to quite a few compatriots staying in Paris and, learning of his appointment with Sanson, many had invited themselves along too.

'On the way there,' Appert wrote, 'Lord Durham asked me if it would be possible to buy a sheep and have it guillotined. I told him that would give rise to unfavourable remarks, and he did not press the matter. When we reached the rue des Marais I saw there were quite fifty of us, so I went into the hangman's house alone. He was dressed in black as on official occasions, and led us all to the painter's place by the St. Martin canal where the deadly instrument was kept.'

The guillotine had been erected in the middle of the courtyard, and the crowd of ladies and gentlemen pressed round it to hear Henri Sanson explain its functioning and see him work it. Most of his audience had been drawn there because of the notoriety achieved by the Sansons in London since Madame Tussaud had put the waxwork model of 'The execution of Louis XVI' on show. This group contained Charles-Henri and his assistants, as well as the King beneath 'the actual guillotine', and to heighten the scene Madame Tussaud had dressed the executioner in the revolutionary garb, red bonnet and all — which was more effective than the black frock-coat and hat that he had really worn. The same deliberate error was made in many contemporary engravings of the scene.

To demonstrate the powerfulness of the knife, Henri Sanson used it on trusses of straw. It weighed 15 pounds, but in addition had a bronze weight of some 65 pounds attached to it.

A man of odd renown was there helping Henri and his son with their explanations. This was Vidocq, the ex-convict who had become head of the secret police and who founded the Sûreté, the French Scotland Yard. Benjamin Appert thought a lot of him, and approved his schemes for the rehabilitation of released convicts. It was almost impossible for them to get honest employment. On leaving prison, a convict was given an identity-card — every French person had to have one, and could not travel about the country without it. Any employer asked to see an applicant's identity-card before engaging him, and on discovering that he was an ex-convict — those who had been imprisoned at Toulon, for instance, had yellow cards — automatically refused to take him on. Inevitably, ex-convicts drifted back to the underworld and committed fresh robberies and crimes. Vidocq was well aware of this tragic problem; he had only found a way out of it himself by working for the police. He knew every ex-convict, and when one seemed to justify the trouble Vidocq mentioned him to Appert, who used all his influence to get the man a job.

Appert had asked Vidocq to come to the Sanson house in order to introduce him to the executioner's titled visitors. Appert, however, later wrote in his Memoirs that Vidocq's commentary on the guillotine aroused in him 'the deepest repugnance; though Lord Durham and Lord Ellice and all the others found it most interesting.'

Appert often had people prominent in the world of arts and science to dinner at his house at Neuilly. Knowing this, Lord Durham and his two compatriots suggested he should invite Sanson to dinner with them. Appert was not at all keen, but at their urging 'he went and invited Sanson for the following Saturday.

The public executioner stared at him in amazement.

'Don't you want to come?' said Appert.

'Why — yes! But my son, who often takes my place, would be delighted to have the same honour.'

The philanthropist could hardly refuse at this point, and invited Henri-Clément as well. Then several of the English standing around asked to be included in the somewhat unusual dinner-party, and in the end Appert found himself obliged to make two occasions of it.

The two Sansons and Vidocq were of course guests at both dinner-parties. The others present on the first occasion were

Lords Durham and Ellice, Sir John Bowring, Honoré de Balzac, Alexandre Dumas, and a few writers of less renown. Appert had thought of including Victor Hugo, but decided not to bring together the executioner and the man who had poured such scorn upon him in the preface to 'The Last Day of a Condemned Man'. The second dinner-party included some English and the sociologist, Charles Fourier, who had founded centres of communal living, and his follower, Victor Considérant; the mesmerizer, Doctor Chapelain, and the physician, Camille Broussais.

To ensure that his guests ate well, Appert hired an excellent chef named Gillard. This man had eaten prison bread in the past, having been arrested and tried together with Lemoine for the murder of a servant-woman while burglaring a house. Lemoine had admitted murdering the woman and said his friend Gillard was innocent of it. The jury had doubted this, but there was no proof against Gillard and he had been acquitted. The two Sansons shared the doubts of the jury, and in guillotining Lemoine had believed they were aiding an injustice in favour of Gillard.

Benjamin Appert had followed the trial closely and was convinced of Gillard's innocence; to demonstrate this, he employed his services as cook on special occasions. 'I thus had at my table the executioner who would have been called on to cut off the innocent cook's head,' Appert wrote when describing the first of the two dinner-parties. 'When the guests were told Gillard's story they asked me to send for him at the end of the meal so that he could have coffee with us, and thus see we were convinced of the rightness of his acquittal. He was greatly touched by our concern for him, and his tears rolled freely. The two executioners looked dumbfounded; they stared at Gillard as though fearing they had already executed innocent men.'

One of the guests asked Henri-Clément what his feelings were when he had to guillotine someone. 'I'm very upset when I'm informed, and full of relief when the thing's over,' he replied. 'After all, it's our duty; there are such great villains about! My father, like me, was very doleful over the poor young men of La Rochelle, who were guilty only of letting themselves be led.'

Balzac spoke very little during the meal; he seemed rather

embarrassed. Four or five years previously, when gathering material for the *Memoirs relative to the history of the French Revolution* supposedly written by Charles-Henri Sanson, Balzac had interviewed Henri on several occasions and been given many useful details by him. Balzac had no desire for his anonymous collaboration in this early hack-work to be mentioned; and fearing Henri Sanson might reveal something of it, kept out of the conversation at table and concentrated on his food.

Vidocq, on the other hand, scarcely stopped talking. Reminiscences flowed from him, much more than from the two Sansons who were daunted by the presence of the English *milords*.

'These grand seigneurs make me nervous,' Henri whispered to Appert, who had placed him on his left at table.

Vidocq, sitting on Appert's other side, overheard this. 'He's a good fellow, is Monsieur Sanson,' he said to his host. 'But eating at the same table as him gives me a queer feeling.'

'Me too,' retorted Appert. He might have added to himself: 'On my left is the public executioner, and on my right the most notorious of ex-convicts. Luckily I've two honourable peers of the House of Lords sitting opposite me!'

At the second gathering the two Sansons were more convivial. The English present were of less importance than the 'grand seigneurs'. Towards the end of the meal, Doctor Chapelain explained his belief in hypnotism. 'He put one of the men to sleep, and the replies he obtained from him were really extraordinary,' Appert wrote afterwards. Was it one of the Sansons? From the context, that seems possible; but we do not know for certain. A pity Appert was not more precise!

Henri Sanson had been most flattered by the two Lords visiting him and by the invitations to dinner, and when he learnt that Durham had suggested it all he turned to him — this was during the first dinner-party — and said, thinking to please him: '*Milord*, I should like to show my gratitude. In future I'll send you, through Monsieur Appert, the clothes worn at their death by guillotined persons whose trial has aroused much interest.'

This unusual promise cast a chill over the table. Lord Durham could hardly spurn it, and nodded his acceptance.

So in the following years one of Sanson's assistants took the clothes worn on the scaffold by Lacenaire, Fieschi, and Alibaud to Appert's house at Neuilly, for the philanthropist to send them to England. On each occasion Appert gave 15 francs to the assistant, the sorry clothing being part of his perquisites, but took good care it was not forwarded to Lord Durham!

The trials of those three — Lacenaire, Fieschi, and Alibaud — certainly 'aroused much interest'. Could it really have been to please Lord Durham and *to show his gratitude* that Henri Sanson sent along their clothes? The elderly executioner was not stupid; he was well aware that possession of an assassin's apparel gave no pleasure to an honest man. His idea, with some sense of grim humour, was probably to pay the noble lord out for his prying curiosity.

If customs connected with the gibbet had applied also to the guillotine, Sanson would not have been able to send Lacenaire's clothes to Appert. When the rope broke under the weight of a man being hanged, he was pardoned. And, if the newspapers of the day are to be believed, the knife stuck in the grooves before reaching Lacenaire's neck. Three times the executioner tried to guillotine the assassin, and each time the knife stuck in the same place. Lacenaire made a superhuman effort; although strapped to the plank, he managed to turn his head and look at the knife, which was red with the blood of his accomplice, Avril, guillotined first. He stared up horror-stricken at the frightful steel triangle. Then it came down completely.

Henri-Clément wrote to several of the papers protesting against their accounts of the execution. 'The incident of the knife has been imagined just to give a more dramatic end to a case in which many strings have already been pulled.' This was an allusion to attempts at getting Lacenaire's sentence commuted to one of imprisonment. Henri-Clément ended his letter with the statement: 'Nothing out of the ordinary occurred when Lacenaire's turn came, and he was executed with no more difficulty than his accomplice, Avril.'

But not one of the newspapers inserted his denial.

Henri Sanson was 69 when, in 1836, he retired and gave place to his son. Henri-Clément had to guillotine one person, a man named David, and then came the threefold execution of Fieschi and his two accomplices, Pépin and Morey. These three had tried to assassinate the King, Louis-Philippe, when he was reviewing troops in the Boulevard du Temple on the sixth anniversary of the July Revolution. They had used an 'infernal machine' with fifty barrels to it, all fired simultaneously; Fieschi had thought it out, Pépin had paid for it, and Morey had constructed it. Louis-Philippe escaped without a scratch, but 18 people were killed and 32 wounded.

The three condemned men were taken to the St. Jacques Barrier in three carriages; Henri-Clément and two assistants following in another. Troops drawn up in a semi-circle kept the crowd from the scaffold. Five minutes were sufficient to guillotine the three; and then Henri-Clément had great difficulty in retaining Fieschi's coat, for screaming women tried to snatch it from him. These fierce supporters of the revolutionaries wanted souvenirs of the three guillotined men — their clothing, the ropes that had bound their hands, or even tufts of their hair. The police succeeded in getting Henri-Clément away from these furies, but only when he had let them have most of what they wanted. He tossed the coats and belongings of Pépin and Morey to one of the women, and the crowd carried them away shouting its hatred of the regime.

Next day, one of Sanson's assistants knocked at Appert's door and handed him Fieschi's coat. The philanthropist took it, then burnt it in his stove.

The last item of clothing sent to Neuilly had belonged to another would-be regicide. Alibaud had tried to shoot the King with a gun made to look like a walking-stick, but it did no more harm to Louis-Philippe than had Fieschi's multiple weapon. Less than fifty people gathered by the St. Jacques Barrier to see Alibaud die. His modest side-arm was not in the same category as a fifty-barrelled machine-gun; without a single victim, there was no interest from the masses! On the scaffold, which had only a few gendarmes ranged round it, Alibaud's last words were said scornfully to Henri-Clément. 'Is so much ceremony needed to kill a man?'

At about this time a journalist, having heard of the English going to see the public executioner and of the two dinner-parties given by Appert, also went and called on Henri Sanson. His name was James Rousseau and he was an assistant-editor on the *Gazette des Tribunaux*, a police-court periodical. He described his interview with the executioner later on, in 1844. His impression of Henri Sanson was rather different from Appert's; whereas the latter found Henri to be not unsociable, Rousseau reported him as being very conscious of the gulf between him and ordinary people.

'I was shown into a small, low-ceilinged room,' Rousseau wrote of his visit, 'where a man who looked about 60 was playing the piano. He had a gentle face with a calm, open expression; his tall build, his fine bald head and regular features gave him the air of a patriarch. He was in fact 70 years of age.

'His son was in the room too, a man of about 38 with a timid, mild manner, and there was also a girl of 15 or so who looked most lively and genteel. She was the younger man's daughter!'

The journalist had a long talk with Henri Sanson, and gave his impressions of it: 'Monsieur Sanson did not hide from himself the horror of the position that fate had given him. He put up with it, not as a man disdaining the consequences but, wisely, as someone aware of what he stood for.'

Having the word 'duty' constantly in mind, Sanson fulfilled his conscientiously; which 'restored him in his own eyes, never letting him forget the gulf that society had put between it and him.'

An incident gave Rousseau an indication of Henri Sanson's awareness of this gulf. At that period cigarettes had not been thought of, and most men took snuff. It was polite custom, when one took a pinch of snuff, to offer some to any man one happened to be with — just as today one offers a cigarette. During Rousseau's interview with Henri Sanson the latter kept opening his snuff-box and taking a pinch, but never once offered it to his visitor. However, Rousseau realised the other's scruples and did not take offence. But when he drew out his own snuff-box he automatically held it out to Sanson, forgetting in the heat of conversation just who and what he was. And Henri put up a hand in refusal 'with an expression on his face impossible to described'.

'He made me feel uneasy. Poor man! He'd remembered something that had stained his fingers with blood.'

Rousseau's final touch to his depiction of Henri Sanson was that when he held out his hand to take leave of Sanson, the executioner stepped back and stared at him 'with an astonished and almost bewildered air'.

This is a very different Henri Sanson from the one at table with the English peers!

Whom are we to believe — the journalist or the philanthropist?

Both, no doubt; for Vidocq was present at the gatherings described by Appert, and the police-chief had the knack of making the public executioner unbend. Vidocq's sallies were usually well-directed and shot home. At Appert's second dinner-party, Henri Sanson was recounting how his father had given up office in his favour and had remarked to him, 'You'll be left alone anyway, no one will poke their nose into your affairs.'

'Except the people whose heads you'll cut off!' exclaimed Vidocq. 'Your father ought to have added that!'

'It's nothing to joke about, Monsieur Vidocq. What I'm saying is a fact.'

'Unfortunately!'

Henri then took on the grave and distant manner that James Rousseau was to meet with, and said in a low voice to his host, 'It's obvious this man has never associated with respectable people. His behaviour isn't like mine.'

Henri Sanson, of course, had 'associated' with people like Marie-Antoinette, had stroked Mrs. Elliot's neck and bound Lavoisier's wrists. Whereas Vidocq knew little better company than that of assassins and harlots.

Henri Sanson had even stood up to Napoleon. At least, so he

told one of his English visitors, Henry E. Marquand, who was a teacher in Guernsey and an ardent supporter of the abolition of the death penalty. He called on the Sansons during a visit to Paris, but found the two men were out. However, he was asked in by a 'charming young girl' who chatted with him while waiting for Henri and his son to return home. The name of Victor Hugo came into the conversation, but that was a tricky subject. Mademoiselle Sanson, very much the hostess, avoided it by sitting down to sing and play the piano.

Henri Sanson came in. Marquand wrote that he was 'a fine-looking man, nearly six feet tall, with a gentle, handsome face, but very pale; quite the air of a gentleman.'

Monsieur de Paris trotted out his reminiscences for his visitor. And this was one of them:

It happened in the days of Napoleon. At the top of the rue Royale workmen were building a 'Temple of Glory' (now the Madeleine church). Henri Sanson, out for a stroll along the boulevards, wandered into the site; he was watching the masons at work when a lot of noise was suddenly heard in the street, and then a voice ordered, 'Outside, everybody! The Emperor is coming!'

The order applied to the onlookers, not to the workmen, whom Napoleon had come to inspect. He strode into the site, booted and spurred and clutching his riding-whip, followed by a group of high officials.

Henri Sanson had never seen the Emperor at close quarters. So instead of clearing off he hid behind a pillar, holding the book he had brought with him in his hand. Suddenly he felt someone grasp him by the collar. It was Roustam, the famous Mameluke, Napoleon's watchdog; he saw spies and assassins everywhere, and brought Henri to the Emperor.

'What are you doing here?' Napoleon said to him.

'Sire, I was looking and admiring.'

'What were you looking at? What were you admiring?'

'Your Majesty first, and then your temple.'

'What's that you're reading?'

'It's a volume of Racine.'

Napoleon snatched the book from him, opened it and saw it did not camouflage a weapon. Reassured, he said, 'Who are you?'

'Sire, I am Sanson, the public executioner.'

Napoleon dropped the book in disgust and walked away. But he at once turned back and asked Henri, 'Were you performing those functions in 1793?'

'Yes, Sire.'

Napoleon hesitated a moment. 'And if,' he then said, fixing Henri with his eyes, 'if there were a reaction against me? If some wretches dared to . . .?' He left the question unfinished.

Henri Sanson, telling the story to Henry Marquand, said: 'I made a deep bow to the Emperor and replied, 'Sire, I executed Louis XVI.' Meaning, of course, that if ordered I'd do as much to him. Napoleon lost colour, and snapped at me to pick up my book and go.'

What is to be made of this story? One detail of it at least is false — Henri Sanson did not execute Louis XVI. He was indeed in the Place de la Révolution that day, but standing in the ranks of the National Guard and not on the scaffold.

But does that mean the rest of it is just as false? That Henri made it up to impress his visitor with his audacity? This would give a very different idea of Henri Sanson from those presented by Appert and James Rousseau. How could the man who was so timid in the presence at table of the 'grand seigneurs', Lords Durham and Ellice, have stood up to the all-powerful Napoleon twenty years earlier? But perhaps it was just because he *was* twenty years younger at the time.

The year 1840 began with a trial that Henri-Clément, who felt increasing repulsion for 'the machine', thought of with dread. His father was 73 and in ill-health, and left control of the assistants to Henri-Clément. To forget his responsibilities he began to frequent houses of ill-fame and gambling-dens. His losses at the tables led to quarrels with his wife and his parents. But he took little notice, considering that at 41 he was free to do as he liked. He had been obliged to take over functions that he detested, so at least he could get right away from them whenever possible.

On January 31st he heard that the revolutionary leader, Auguste Blanqui, had been sentenced to death for organising a riot. Henri-Clément asked himself with anguish whether he would have to guillotine the man and so become odious to the Republican party. Fortunately, the King commuted the sentence to imprisonment on the island of Mont St. Michel; and Henri-Clément gave a sigh of relief.

Then, later in the year, the name of Bonaparte was much in the news. One of Louis-Philippe's sons, the Prince de Joinville, sailed for St. Helena to bring the Emperor's body back to Paris; and the Emperor's nephew, Louis-Napoleon, landed at Boulogne in an attempt to overthrow the King. But it was unsuccessful, and Louis-Napoleon was captured and brought to Paris to stand trial.

This was the second time Louis-Napoleon had tried to seize power, and Henri-Clément was terrified that he might be called upon to guillotine a Bonaparte. He read in one newspaper, *La Presse*, these frightening words:

'The disgusting thing is the ingratitude in forgetting that once already the royal pardon has been given to a crime that could have been punished with the utmost severity, and which Napoleon himself would have made its perpetrators pay dearly for within twenty-four hours.'

Old Henri Sanson took a turn for the worse just then, and died a few days later, in the evening of August 18th, 1840. Only two or three friends, besides the family, were at his funeral. He was buried in the Sanson tomb at Montmartre cemetery, which was still without a headstone; even the base of the tomb was bare of any inscription.

So the dreaded responsibility for the office so long in the Sanson family fell entirely on Henri-Clément's shoulders. Would he have to begin in the official position by guillotining Prince Louis-Napoleon? By adding the execution of a member of the Imperial family to those of the Bourbons performed by his father and grandfather? It was a horrible thought.

Great was Henri-Clément's relief when he heard that Napoleon's nephew had been sentenced to life detention.

CHAPTER NINE

Henri-Clément, the Last

FOR NEARLY four months Henri-Clément put off claiming his father's office. But what else was there for him to do, at the age of 41, when all he had learnt as a profession was how to decapitate his fellow-beings speedily? Towards the end of November he applied to the authorities, and on December 1st was officially appointed public executioner.

Physically, he took after his mother rather than the Sanson side of the family, being much shorter than his father. He was 'a big, clean-shaven man, with the head of a Rabelaisian monk and a chin shining from all the cold-cream he kept rubbing in five or six times a day.' That at least is how he was later described in *Le Figaro* by Georges Grison, a journalist who knew him well.

Henri-Clément was better educated than his male forbears, and made no mistakes in his spelling; like them, he was fond of music and could play the piano. In addition, he was something of a connoisseur of painting, and collected pictures; without disclosing who he was, he frequently visited artists' studios. If it were not for him often seeking distraction in disreputable haunts, he might have been taken for a rather haughty, blasé man of the world with a love of women and gambling, squandering the money he had inherited.

He spent little time at home, and was a constant source of worry to his wife and his mother. The latter was 64 when she became a widow, and Virginie was then 42.

The family earnings were diminishing; for its new head had dropped the quack medicine, and his salary had been reduced from ten to eight thousand francs. The few people he had to guillotine were still required to pay the cost of the execution

— 'the guillotine comes very dear,' groaned the wretched hero of Hugo's 'Last Day of a Condemned Man' — but when guillotined criminals had nothing to leave, the executioner did not get his expenses.

However, the investments made by Henri ensured that his son did not lack money. Dividends came in regularly, and dowries were ready for Henri-Clément's two daughters. He could consider himself secure from any disaster.

This erring husband was a good father. He did not think the family house had the right aspect to help his daughters find husbands. Cheerfulness was what attracted suitors, and the house had a much too gloomy appearance. So masons, carpenters, and painters were called in, and soon the forbidding entrance courtyard was converted into a glass-enclosed hall furnished with comfortable armchairs and having a polished oak door.

James Rousseau, the journalist who had visited the Sansons in 1836, went to see the alterations in 1844. He wrote then: 'The present executioner is very different from his father. When speaking of his profession and details appertaining to it, he does not show the embarrassment, disquiet, or shame that could be noticed in his predecessor. He speaks of his functions with remarkable ease.'

From 1840 to 1847 these functions consisted of guillotining 18 people. This small figure — less than three a year — shows the success the abolitionist campaign was having. The times when the Place de Grève had its daily blood-bath were long past. The courts were more understanding, the juries showed a clemency in keeping with the march of progress. Even in 1836 Léon Faucher had written in the *Revue de Paris*: 'The scaffold now appears in our public squares only on rare occasions, and then as a spectacle that justice is ashamed of showing.'

Henri-Clément approved of such observations. He himself no longer directed operations but let Piot, his chief assistant, take charge of everything. Once, however, he carried out an execution personally, at the request of the person chiefly concerned. This man, whose name was Salmon, made his appeal to Henri-Clément more or less in these words: 'I know your family; I know you, I know that you are good and humane. I count on you to ease my last moments.'

Henri-Clément was deeply affected by this, and promised to take charge at the ordeal. He kept his word; the man died thanking him.

That year, 1843, the executioner, his wife and his mother, had what was perhaps the happiest moment of their lives. The elder daughter married — and she married a doctor. Yes, a Paris doctor became Sanson's son-in-law.

James Rousseau congratulated Sanson, but not without showing some surprise at such a strange union. Henri-Clément retorted quite simply: 'Now just consider the matter. In order to save a human body, a surgeon is often obliged to sacrifice a diseased member. When the social body has a gangrenous member, isn't it right to sacrifice that?'

'But,' replied the journalist, 'there's a great deal of difference in the two sacrifices.'

'Certainly — in the size of the knife!'

That knife gave Henri-Clément an opportunity for another verbal sally. Since Lord Durham had started the fashion, many English tourists came to Sanson's door. He invited them to sit down in the hall, and chatted amiably with them.

These English nearly always asked to see the guillotine. Then Henri-Clément took them to the shed on the Quai de Valmy where it was stored, and worked it using trusses of straw.

One day — so wrote Victor Hugo, who got the story from one of the executioner's assistants — an English family comprising the parents and three pretty, pink-and-white daughters expressed the usual desire, and Sanson took them to the painter's place and worked the machine for them several times.

But one of the daughters, the youngest and the prettiest, was still not satisfied. Henri-Clément had to explain to her in the greatest detail how condemned prisoners were prepared for the guillotine — the condemned's toilet, as it was called. Then she asked Sanson what happened on the scaffold — how was the condemned person tied?

The executioner explained the frightful business, and added, 'We call that *enfourner* — trussing up.'

'Well, Monsieur Sanson,' said the girl. 'I should like you to *enfourner* me. I want to be able to say I've been attached to the guillotine.'

Sanson gave a start of horror. He tried to dissuade her, but the girl persisted. He appealed to her parents, but they only said, 'As that's what she wants, you'd better do it.'

So he tied her legs together, bound her arms behind her back, placed her on the plank and strapped her to it.

That was as much as he intended. 'No, no,' she said. 'There's still something else.'

Then Henri-Clément let the plank go forward, and fixed the girl's head in the fatal aperture. Only then did she declare herself satisfied.

When Henri-Clément was telling this story later, he said, 'I saw the moment coming when she would say to me — *There's still something. Release the knife.*'

According to Victor Hugo, Henri-Clément took money for demonstrating the guillotine to his visitors, and Hugo was no doubt right. The Sanson capital was fast disappearing; Henri-Clément's gambling, running after women, and buying of pictures, were leading him to ruin. For a time he was able to sell the shareholdings inherited from his father, but when they had all gone he began to get into debt, signing moneylenders' bills. The time came when he was reduced to pawning furniture and family heirlooms, which he got out if he had a good win at gambling or when he received his salary; and pawned them again later. Once he was drawn into this vicious circle he found it increasingly difficult to escape, and the gap in his financial situation widened. His creditors started to threaten him with 'Clichy'.

This was the name popularly given to the debtors' prison, because it stood in the rue de Clichy, at the corner of the present rue du Cardinal Mercier. A stay in 'Clichy' was not considered a disgrace; many well-known people spent a period there, Alexandre Dumas among them. It had separate quarters for men and women — not in prison cells, but in well-furnished, clean and airy rooms, centrally-heated by a large stove. From some of the windows the detainees could see the Tivoli Gardens and catch the strains of the dance orchestra. If the person seized for debt was wealthy — for one could be wealthy in a debtors' prison! — he took his meals in the restaurant of the establishment. Otherwise the creditor responsible for the detention paid 30 francs a month for his debtor's keep. There was a reading-room, games of skittles in the yard, messengers to run errands about the city, and a post-office; and visits could always be made by friends and relatives — such were the advantages of this unusual prison, which sheltered all kinds and conditions of men.

They were not conducted there by gendarmes or law officers. One does not treat bad payers as though they are criminals! A special body of men called *recors* was employed for the purpose — the equivalent of bailiff's men — and their task was sometimes made more delicate by having to take pretty women to 'Clichy'. Several of these *recors* had themselves spent periods in the prison, as debtors.

Messager's light opera, *Véronique,* has a character who becomes a *recors* — though it was written in 1898, long after the debtors' prison had ceased to exist — and he gaily sings how the only way he could get out of 'Clichy' was by becoming a bailiff's man.

These *recors* were forbidden by law from seizing their victims outside Paris, and in the capital itself between six in the evening and six in the morning. So it was usual for sued debtors to leave the city at dawn and stay away until dusk. The village of Batignolles, then just outside Paris, specialised in catering for these daily visitors; its restaurants supplied meals at moderate prices, and the hotels let rooms by the day — literally, for the clients did not sleep in them. Towards evening, they went and waited by the Clichy or Monceau gate until six o'clock struck, when they surged into Paris, greeted by the laughs and jeers of provincial and foreign visitors who looked upon them as a tourist attraction and pointed out well-known figures thus avoiding being put in the debtors' prison.

For months, Henri-Clément Sanson was one of these 19th-century commuters. Dogged by the agent of a pitiless creditor, he was forced to stay away from his wife and family all day long. Fortunately, as the courts were condemning very few criminals, his absences went unnoticed in high quarters.

However, a morning came when he had to perform his grisly function. And the *recors* was waiting for such an opportunity. The discreet agent hired a closed cab, set off behind the executioner, and followed him to the St. Jacques Barrier.

The condemned man was named Lecomte; like Fieschi and Alibaud, he had fired at the King and missed. Lecomte belonged to no political party. He was the head ranger of Fontainebleau forest, and had twice been fined by his superior for brutality towards his men; 20 francs had been stopped each time from his annual salary of 300. This annoyed him so much that he gave up his job and applied for a pension. But the forest of Fontainebleau was Louis-Philippe's private property; as it did not belong to the Crown, Lecomte was not a civil servant and had no claim to a pension, and this was pointed out to him.

The ex-forest ranger got so angry that he wrote to the King. No reply. He wrote a second and a third time, with no better result. Maddened and frustrated, Lecomte decided to kill his late employer — the King. He chose the moment when Louis-Philippe arrived at the château of Fontainebleau with his family in an open carriage. He fired twice from the top of a wall, and missed. He might have killed the Queen or one of her grand-children; but he did not touch one of them, and was arrested after a man-hunt in the park.

The Upper House, again restored to its function of a law court, took five days to examine his case. After the prosecution and the defence had been heard, each member of the House rose in turn to give his decision. The first 32 speakers voted for sentence of death. The next drew all eyes upon him — he was Victor Hugo, created peer the previous year. After paying tribute to the public-prosecutor, the Chancellor, and to those peers who had given their vote, he went on to say:

'For 18 years my ideas on irreparable punishments have been clear and explicit. These ideas are already well known to you. As a writer, I have published them; as a politician I will, with God's help, apply them. I abhor irreparable punishment on principle; in this particular case, there is no place for it at all. Pierre Lecomte, a lonely, mean-spirited man, was bound to become savage and morose. An attempt on the life of the King, on the life of a father — and just when he is surrounded by his family; an attempt on the lives of a group of women and children, death hurled blindly — adding a score of possible crimes to the one intended — that is his deed! A ghastly deed! Now let us look at the motive — 20 francs stopped from a year's salary, a resignation that had been accepted, and three letters left unanswered. How can we fail to be struck by the great difference between the two? In considering these two extremes — the enormity of the crime and the pettiness of the motive — it is obvious to me that reason is lacking, that this guilty man, this assassin, this wild, solitary man, this terrified and ferocious being is a madman. I vote for life imprisonment.'

Only two other peers voted with Hugo. By 229 to 3, Lecomte was delivered up to the executioner.

From the scaffold, soon after dawn on June 8th, 1846, Henri-Clément noticed a *closed* cab, a vehicle not often seen in the summer. Inside, the *recors* was waiting and watching. He was very considerate, allowing Henri-Clément to direct proceedings, to attend to the taking down of the guillotine and the transport of Lecomte's body to the Clamart cemetery. The cab followed behind.

When Sanson returned home the hired cab was still following. It stopped in front of the door, the *recors* rang the bell and went in.

Twenty minutes later he came out again with his prisoner. Henri-Clément was carrying a suitcase. And the debtors' prison had got another lodger.

There was no end to his protests. How could the public do

without him, an instrument of justice? But his creditors were not impressed. No money, no freedom. And the executioner remained in 'Clichy'.

Not for long, though. Someone — he or one of his creditors — had a brilliant idea. Why not pawn his guillotine? It was his property, he could do what he liked with it. This was both a pleasant and a practical idea.

So Henri-Clément, accompanied by the *recors*, went and collected his famous machine from the painter's shed. Loading it on an upholsterer's van that he had hired, he took it to his principal creditor.

'When you've paid me 3,800 francs,' said the latter, 'I'll let you have your machine back.'

Several months went by. But Henri-Clément was not free from anxiety, even though freed from prison. One day the dreaded blow fell, in the form of the usual summons: 'The executioner of criminal sentences is to be without fail at the Palais de Justice tomorrow, etc.,' He received this, as was the custom, the day before the execution was to be carried out. Panic-stricken, he rushed off to the holder of his apparatus and pleaded for it to be lent to him for a morning. But the creditor was adamant and refused point-blank.

Henri-Clément was obliged to go with his tail between his legs and confess everything to the public-prosecutor. The latter, Monsieur Hébert, had just been given the Ministry of Justice; but as his successor had not yet been appointed, he was temporarily combining the two offices. It was therefore impossible for the public-prosecutor, even if he had wanted to, to hide the follies of the executioner from the Minister. Monsieur Hébert advanced Henri-Clément the 3,800 francs needed to get the guillotine out of pawn.

The next day, March 18th, 1847, Henri-Clément guillotined his last victim. The same evening he was relieved of his office. And the Sanson dynasty of public executioners had come to an end.

But it was not the end of Henri-Clément's misfortunes...

There were 18 candidates for his vacant post, which went to
Joseph Heinderech, the son of an ex-public executioner at Mâcon.
He went to live in the rue de la Folie-Regnault, in the east of
Paris.

There was much less competition to acquire the Sanson house,
which was put up for sale by Henri-Clément's creditors. Admittedly, it needed someone with strong nerves, not afraid of ghosts.
Eventually a purchaser was found, a man who had been a currier
and was said to have sold straps for the guillotine. His name was
Edouard Plouvier, and at the time he bought the Sanson house
he had left the leather trade and was contributing poetry and
serials to a periodical called *Le Musée des Familles*. Edouard
Plouvier became one of the popular dramatists of his time —
inspired, perhaps, by the spectres in his new home — and had
more than thirty of his plays performed. One of them, a vaudeville
written in collaboration, had a title that was significant — 'Hands
Off The Axe!'

The late owner of the house disappeared into the country with
his wife, mother, and the unmarried daughter. Not to the house
at Brunoy, for that too had been seized and sold to satisfy
creditors. But it is difficult to say just where they did retire to, so
many precautions did they take to conceal their real identity.

They returned to Paris in 1857, by which time the Louis-
Napoleon whom Henri-Clément had feared he might have to
guillotine was solidly in power and reigning over the Second
Empire. The Sansons' financial situation was obviously much
improved, for Henri-Clément bought a house in the village of
Epinettes, which did not become part of Paris until three years
later. Had he and his wife inherited some money from her
parents? It is quite likely. The new home of the Sansons was
No. 10, rue St. Jean, a small turning off the Avenue de Clichy.[1]
They occupied a large apartment in this five-storeyed building,
and let the rest of it to seven tenants, including those who had
the three shops on the ground floor. In those days, the rents thus

---

[1]) The building is still standing, though dilapidated. Two shops and a restaurant
take up the ground floor, and the rest is lived in.

obtained were well worth having; the Sansons had a good steady income.

Henri-Clément's wife died at the end of March, 1860. He buried her in the family vault in Montmartre cemetery, less than a quarter of a mile from the house; and this was the occasion when the tombstone that can still be seen was erected. Due to Henri-Clément, the grave was no longer anonymous. He had the names of the three already buried in it engraved on the tombstone, and underneath Charles-Henri Sanson's were put the words:

'Lamented by his grandson and family,
who put up this tombstone.'
and Henri Sanson's was followed by:
'He was the benefactor of all his family,
who still pray for him.'

Henri-Clément still had his old mother living with him — she was well into her 80s — and his youngest daughter, who was getting on for 40.

At about this time a music-hall dancer calling herself Mademoiselle Sanson was having a great success at the Salle Barthélemy — a success largely due to the public's belief that she was indeed a member of the notorious family. An executioner's daughter or grand-daughter showing her legs was no ordinary spectacle! But there is nothing to prove the public was right. Although a dancer can still be graceful and talented when nearing 40, the story seems a bit thick to be believed. A macabre touch to her act was the fact that the Salle Barthélemy had previously been named 'The Turnip Field' — which was what the Paris underworld called the cemetery at Clamart where guillotined criminals were buried. 'You're ripe for the turnip field,' an unsuccessful criminal would be told by his fellows. 'Bah! I'll get a squint at Sanson's girl there.'

In 1862, Henri-Clément came back into the public eye in more spectacular fashion than his presumed or actual daughter. That was the year the *Memoirs of the Sansons* was published. As already mentioned in the present introduction, Henri-Clément provided the material for the 'Memoirs', and two journalists wrote it up for him. The publisher sold 80,000 copies, and paid the ex-public executioner 30,000 francs (roughly equivalent to £6,000 or about $17,000 today). The book was discussed in all the papers and periodicals. It was, in short, a great success.

Henri-Clément must have been very pleased. He believed the book would restore the Sanson line in the good opinion of the public.

His mother, Marie-Louise, died in 1866 at the ripe old age of 90. Being the wife and the mother of public executioners keeps one going. Her name was added to those on the Sanson tombstone, with the following lines:

'Rest in peace, worthy and loving mother.

You did nothing but good,

May God reward you by your acts.'

In 1871, the Prussians' victory over the French and its consequences led to the setting-up of another Paris Commune. During the subsequent siege of the capital by French Government troops, the Sanson family was again in the limelight. Not as in 1793, during the first Commune, in the glare of day and on the bloodstained scaffold of the guillotine. No, the Sansons now belonged to a forgotten and outdated past; but they were dragged out of their grave, though without anyone — and this was the most extraordinary part — realising whose bones were being put on view.

The insurrection was in arms not only against the French regular troops, but also against accepting defeat by the Prussians, against capitalism, the death penalty, the Church and its priests. The Communards opposition to the death penalty — which they themselves, however, dealt out with bullets — led men of the 137th Battalion of the National Guard to break into the home of Heinderech, Sanson's successor, and loot it. They dragged out the guillotine and burnt it in the Place Voltaire, by the famous writer's statue.

The Commune's attacks on the Church, against 'its superstitions and its incense-swingers,' had a brutal repercussion on the history of the Sansons — their family vault was cracked open. In April, defilers of churches started breaking up the stone flooring in St. Laurent's, and came across a short flight of steps between the churchwarden's pew and a small chapel in the north aisle of the nave. Enchanted with this discovery, thinking it would lead to some treasure or evidence against the clergy, these vandals groped their way down the steps and found themselves in a semi-circular vault that had two bricked-up vent-holes. They started digging into the walls and floors with their pickaxes; and saw to their horror, in the dim light, that they were getting out a heap of tibias, thigh-bones, ribs, and grinning skulls.

A chronicler of the Commune, Maxime du Camp, described the result of this discovery: 'They made the most of their find; these human remains were declared to be the bones of young girls whom the priests had lured into the church, and strangled or left to die of hunger, after having used them to gratify their shameful lusts. Illustrated pamphlets showing the corpses in the crypt were sold in the streets, and the hawkers shouted: 'Can you imagine this horrible sight — young women and girls drawn by promises or the hope of pleasure, and waking up here, bound hand and foot, walled up alive! The priest worked his will alone and undisturbed! In the shadows! This is Catholicism at work! Look at it!' '

A municipal councillor named Leroudier arranged an exhibition of the skeletons. His men spread the bones of the early Sansons, all the thirteen buried in the family vault, on a carpet in front of the church door, and placed wooden barriers round them.

But there were seen to be 14, not 13, skeletons! Does this solve the mystery of where Henri Sanson buried his mother, Marie-Anne? When she died — during the Restoration, it will be remembered — her son dared not bury her in Montmartre cemetery, fearing that while the White Terror was in full spate disturbances similar to those at her husband's funeral might occur. It would have taken forty to fifty minutes for the cortege to make its way from the Sanson house in the rue Neuve-Saint-Jean to the cemetery at Montmartre. Instead, Marie-Anne was buried secretively at night.

A proof that her body was placed in St. Laurent's may be provided by the following report that appeared in L'Etoile, the official paper of the Communards, previous to the exhibition of the skeletons outside the church. With a little more attention to truth, the paper said: 'Most of the skeletons are of men, as is shown by the shape of the skull and the bone formation... Enclosed in a cupboard is the skeleton of a young woman still with beautiful fair hair.' But might it not have been the remains of an old woman with white hair in an upright coffin, that the writer of the report had seen? By the flickering light of a candle in the dim vault, and inspired by political passions, he might have taken the coffin for a wooden chest or cupboard, and the white hairs to be fair... And if this *cupboard* did contain the remains of Henri Sanson's mother, it could be explained by some charitable priest having consented, in a time of danger for the Sansons, to a burial which was necessarily furtive and perfunctory, being forbidden by law.

Leroudier, the organiser of this macabre exhibition, wanted to publicise it even more. This sinister impressario wrote an urgent letter to Rigault, the Commune's public-prosecutor, on April 21st:

'A cleverly-written notice to create a public sensation should appear, with explanatory drawings. This lucky find in the church of St. Laurent, if rightly handled, could be worth several centuries of teaching and progress for the whole of humanity.'

Taking the lead himself, Leroudier published an 'Account of enquiries made into the crimes committed in the church of St. Laurent.' In it he asserted that the clergy were nothing but a rabble of sadists and criminals, and quoted a few well-known deviations and added much fiction to the facts, ending with a flourish: 'And you, people of Paris, come in your crowds to see what happens to your wives and daughters in the hands of these vile creatures... Guard this charnel-house, for a century if necessary! It will be the guiding light for humanity until the supreme moment when all the sublime harmonies come together!'

Naturally, those in search of sensation crowded round the bones on display. It would be interesting to know if Henri-Clément was among them; and if so, what could have been the feelings of the poor wretch, especially if the skeleton of the 'young fair-haired woman' was indeed that of his beloved grandmother. But any protest, verbal or written, would have been very risky for the retired executioner. Such a person lies low when a campaign against the death penalty is in progress.

A notice saying 'Stable to let' was put up over the church door.

One day the guard on duty at this gruesome exhibition was shouting out as usual, 'Here are the victims of the lusts of priests!' when a girl passing by gave a laugh and exclaimed, 'Anyone who believes a daft thing like that must be daft himself!' She was immediately arrested, taken to a police-station, and then sent to St. Lazare prison.

An entrance fee of 50 centimes was charged to go down to the vault. There was room for only five or six persons to stand, among the rubble and stones and bits of rotting wood from the coffins. Then the guide would begin: 'It was here that the priests lured their victims. You can see the remains of the cupboards they shut them up in. . .'

It must be admitted that many Communards sincerely believed that such crimes had been committed. No one knew the family vault of the Sansons existed. Even the clergy of St. Laurent's were unaware of it. The parish registers did not go back further than 1810; the previous ones containing records of burials had been destroyed during the French Revolution. Moreover, about ten years before the Commune the vicar of St. Laurent's had been worried by an incident resulting from one of his congregation being locked in the church at night, and then falling asleep. The next day the man claimed to have heard groans around him. The police held an enquiry. They visited the church, questioned clergy and laymen, and instructed that the hero of this mishap should be medically examined. He was found to be subject to hallucinations. So it was not surprising that, ten years later, people whose political passions were roused and who were smarting under defeat, should rake up this old story when they heard of the discovery of the bones. Either, they said, the doctors had been wrong in their diagnosis, or been bribed by the crown or the church. Even the old custom of noble families having their tombs inside the church was not recalled, as the flagstone over the Sanson vault bore no epitaph. That in itself supported the belief in crimes.

When the Commune had been stamped out and order restored, the bones were replaced in the vault and a blank stone slab again sealed the entrance to the stairway.

And the Sansons would never again have been disturbed in their eternal sleep, if workmen early in the 20th century had not made the opening for a stove at the place where they lay. Every winter since then, the bones of the early Sansons have had the sepulchral chill replaced by the pleasant temperature of central heating.

As for the ageing Henri-Clément, he continued living in the building he owned in the rue St. Jean, and to draw the rents, for nearly twenty years after the end of the Commune.

He must certainly have learnt with some interest that one of the first decrees of the Third Republic abolished public executioners in the provinces. Louis Deibler, who had been an assistant to Heinderech, was appointed to the office of *Monsieur de Paris*, becoming the sole public executioner for France and Algeria. He began a new line of executioners, comparatively short though, for only his son followed him in the office.

In 1888, France decided to celebrate the centenary of the Revolution the following year. The Sansons were among the rejects of that tremendous explosion. They had played a big part among the hated auxiliaries of that huge and necessary reform. Old Henri-Clément must have had strange emotions when reading the announcements in the papers of the festivities arranged for 1889. He would be 90 that year.

But he was not destined to celebrate his birthday; nor witness, even from afar, the centenary celebrations. For early in the year his name was added to the tombstone in Montmartre cemetery. There is the last inscription on it:

Henri-Clément SANSON
died January 25th, 1889,
aged 89.

The family grave was tended by Henri-Clément's grand-daughter. She was a familiar figure to the cemetery keepers for thirty years. Every year on January 21st, the anniversary of Louis XVI's death, she placed an armful of flowers on the modest tomb. Then she, too, disappeared; she had retired to the Convent of Nieuil-l'Espoir, near Poitiers.

Now there are only the gentle twitterings of the birds round the tomb of the Sansons, those pitiful and bloodstained actors on the stage of history.

BIBLIOGRAPHY

(In each category, given in the order of use; though most sources were drawn on for material in several chapters).

MEMOIRS, LETTERS, AND PUBLISHED WORKS, CONTEMPORARY WITH THE SANSONS

The Memoirs of the Sansons (Seven generations of executioners, 1688—1847), arranged and edited by H. Sanson, ex-public executioner to the Paris courts. 6 Vols. 1862.

Memoirs relative to the history of the French Revolution, by Sanson, executioner of criminal sentences. Paris, 1829.

Memoirs of the public executioner, of use to the history of Paris during the Terror, edited by A. Grégoire. Paris, 1830.

Armand Fouquier. *Les Causes Célèbres*. 6 Vols. Paris, 1858—67.

Président Henault. *Mémoires.* 1855.

Duc de Saint-Simon. *Mémoires.*

Jacques Peuchet. *Mémoires tirés des archives de la police de Paris, pour servir à l'histoire de la morale et de la police, depuis Louis XIV jusqu'à nos jours.* 6 Vols. Paris, 1838.

Bernard Le Bouyer de Fontenelle. *Eloge de l'anatomiste Littre à l'Académie Française.*

Voltaire. *Le Siècle de Louis XIV.*

Correspondance du Duc d'Avaray avec les magistrats de l'Etat de Bâle. (Archives of the State of Basle — now in the Bib. Nat., Paris.)

L'Art de vérifier les dates des faits historiques, des chartes, des chroniques et autres anciens monuments, etc., De Saint-Allais. 6 Vols. Paris, 1818—25.

Chronique de la Régence, ou Journal de Barbier, avocat au Parlement de Paris. Paris, 1728.

Piganiol de la Force. *Description historique de la Ville de Paris.* Paris, 1765.

Marquis Théophime-Gérard de Lally-Tollendal. *Mémoires et plaidoyers pour la réhabilitation de mon père.* Paris, during reign of Louis XVI.

Pièces originales et procédure du procès de Damiens. Paris, 1757.

L-M Moreau-Christophe. *Code des prisons, ou recueil complet des lois, ordonnances, règlements concernant les prisons, de 1670 jusqu'à nos jours.* 3 Vols. Paris, 1860.

Adolphe Thiers. *Histoire de la Révolution Française.* Paris, 1853.

Louis Blanc. *Histoire de la Révolution Française.* Paris, 1865.

L-Sébastien Mercier. *Tableau de Paris.* Paris, 1780.

L-Sébastien Mercier. *Le Nouveau Paris.* Paris, 1800.

Honoré de Balzac. *Une Messe en 1793.*

Archives Nationales, Paris. Correspondances diverses et rapports (BB3 206—09, 212, 218 and V.1. 540). Minutier central des notaires (Minutes d'actes divers).

Abbé Edgeworth de Firmont. *Memoirs.*

Diurnal de Beaulieu. *Paris sous la Terreur.* Paris, 1797.

Abbé Carrichon. *Anne-Paule-Domi-*

nique de Noailles, Marquise de Montagu. Published in La Nouvelle Revue. Paris, 1865.

Fragments inédits des Mémoires de Dulaure. Revue rétrospective. Paris, 1840.

Comte de Reiset. Livre-Journal de Madame Eloff.

Note de l'architecte Belanger sur l'inhumation des victimes de la Terreur. Paris, 1794.

Emile Campardon. Le Tribunal Révolutionnaire de Paris. Paris, 1865.

Souvenirs de M. Berryer, doyen des avocats de Paris de 1774 à 1778. Brussels, 1839.

Almanach des Honnêtes gens. Paris, 1793.

H. Wallon. Histoire du Tribunal Révolutionnaire de Paris, avec le journal de ses actes. Paris, 1880.

Mrs. Elliot. Memoirs of the French Revolution. London.

Comte de Lamothe-Langon. Les Après-diners de Cambacérès. Paris, 1837.

Anonymous. Procès de la veuve Morin et de sa fille. Paris, 1812.

Choix de Rapports, Opinions et Discours prononcés à la Tribune Nationale, depuis 1789 jusqu'à ce jour. 20 Vols. Paris, 1822.

Barbey d'Aurévilly. Mémoires historiques et littéraires. (containing a short study on the Sansons — published in Les Oeuvres et les Hommes). Paris, 1893.

Archives of the Seine département: Registers of Births, deaths, and marriages. Burial registers of the Cimetière du Nord (Montmartre cemetery).

Benjamin Appert. Dix ans à la cour du roi Louis-Philippe. (Vol. 3). Berlin and Paris, 1846.

Henry E. Marquand. My Visit to Sanson. London, 1865.

Mémoires d'un forçat ou Vidocq dévoilé. Paris, 1838.

Maxime du Camp. L'Attentat Fieschi.

Victor Hugo. Le Dernier Jour d'un Condamné. Paris, 1832.

Victor Hugo. Choses Vues. Paris, 1887.

Victor Hugo raconté par un témoin de sa vie. Paris, 1887.

L-M Moreau-Christophe. Le Monde des Coquins. Paris, 1864.

Vermorel. Les Mystères de la Police. Paris, 1864.

Caussidière, ex-Préfet de police. Mémoires. Paris, 1849.

Gisquet, ex-Préfet de police. Mémoires. Paris, 1840.

Maxime du Camp. Les Convulsions de Paris. Vol. 1 — Les Prisons pendant la Commune. Paris, 1881.

Catulle Mendès. Les 73 journées de la Commune. Paris, 1871.

Adolphe Guillot. Paris qui souffre. Paris, 1887.

Georges Grison. Paris horrible. Paris, 1882.

MODERN PUBLICATIONS

Maurice Soulié. Autour du Régent, 1674—1723. Paris, 1933.

Henri Robert. Les Grands Procès de l'Histoire. 6 Vols. Paris, 1922—28.

Henry Buisson. Crimes célèbres, crimes oubliés. Paris, 1953.

Joseph Calmette. L'Ere Classique. Paris, 1949.

G. Lenotre. *La Guillotine et les exécuteurs des arrêts criminels pendant la Révolution.* Paris, 1908.

G. Lenotre. *Le Tribunal Révolutionnaire.* Paris, 1908.

Jacques Bourgeat. *Guillotine, la mal nommée.* In the Revue, 'Miroir de l'Histoire', June and July, 1955.

Maurice Garçon. *Histoire de la Justice.* Paris.

P. de Vaissière. *La mort du roi.* Paris, 1910.

Marquis de Beaumont. *Captivité et derniers moments de Louis XVI.* Paris, 1892.

Cl. Saint-André. *Madame du Barry.*

John Theodore Tussaud. *The Romance of Madame Tussaud's.* London, 1920.

Claude Cézan. *Le Musée Grevin.* Paris, 1947.

Georges Pair. *Messieurs Sanson, bourreaux.* Paris, 1938. (this book is more fiction than fact).

Charles Simond. *La vie parisienne au 19e siècle.* 3 Vols. Paris, 1901.

L. de Lanzac de Laborie. *Paris sous Napoléon, la Cour et la Ville, la Vie et la Mort.* Paris, 1906.

Emile Chautard. *La Vie Etrange de l'Argot.* Paris, 1934.

Paul Dornain. *De Sanson à Deibler.* Paris, 1934.

Marcel Rousselet. *Histoire de la Justice.* Paris, 1943.

Marcel Rousselet. *Les Souverains devant la Justice, de Louis XVI à Napoléon III.* Paris, 1946.

Jean Savant. *La Vie fabuleuse et authentique de Vidocq.* Paris, 1950.

Georges Benoit-Guyod. *Histoires de Gendarmes.* Paris, 1937.

R. Babize. *Le XVIIIe arrondissement à travers les âges.* Paris.

A. Vanloo et G. Duval. *Libretto of Véronique.* Paris, 1898.

Paul et Victor Margueritte. *La Commune.* Paris, 1904.

Henri d'Alméras. *La vie parisienne pendant le siège et sous la Commune.* Paris, 1927.

NEWSPAPERS AND PERIODICALS

Les Révolutions de Paris (December 26th, 1789). Contre la peine de mort, by Elysée Loustalot.

Moniteur Universel (1793 to 1814).

Le Thermomètre du Jour (January 29th, 1793). Contains a letter by Sanson.

Le Thermomètre du Jour (February 13th, 1793). Anecdote très exacte sur l'exécution de Louis Capet, by Dulaure.

Le Courrier Républicain (1793 and 1794).

Bulletin du Tribunal révolutionnaire (1793 and 1794).

Voilà (September 12th, 1931). Madame Tussaud et la belle endormie, by Paul Gilson.

Gazette des Tribunaux (1815 et seq.).

Journal de l'Empire (for 1812).

Le Temps (August 15th, 1930). La tombe des Sansons, by A. Augustin-Thierry.

La Presse (August 8th, 1840). News items on the arrest of prince Louis-Napoleon.

L'Etoile (April 21st, 1871). Une visite à l'ossuaire de l'église Saint-Laurent.

Le Cri du Peuple (April 26th and 27th, 1871). News items on St. Laurent's church.

Le Petit Journal (June 20th, 1872). News items on the public executioner, Heinderech.

Mercure de France (November 1st, 1951). L'exécution de Louis XVI, by Roger Goulard. (of doubtful value).

WORKS OF REFERENCE

Joseph Michaud. *Biographie Universelle*. Vol. 37.

Robinet, Robert and Le Chaplain. *Dictionnaire de la Révolution et de l'Empire*. Paris, during reign of Louis-Philippe.

A. V. Arnault and others. *Biographie nouvelle des Contemporains*. Paris, 1821—1825.

Rabbe, V. de Boisjolin, and Sainte-Preuve. *Biographie universelle et portative des contemporains ou Dictionnaire historique*. Paris, 1834.

F-X de Feller. *Biographie universelle ou Dictionnaire historique*. Besançon, 1861.

G. Vapereau. *Dictionnaire universel des contemporains*. 1870. ed.

Louis Grégoire. *Dictionnaire encyclopédique d'Histoire, de Biographie et de Géographie*. Paris, 1884.